John Caius, Abraham Fleming

Of Englishe dogges, the diversities, the names,

The natures and the properties. A short treatise written in Latine and

newly drawne into Englishe by Abraham Fleming

John Caius, Abraham Fleming

Of Englishe dogges, the diversities, the names,
The natures and the properties. A short treatise written in Latine and newly drawne into Englishe by Abraham Fleming

ISBN/EAN: 9783337775230

Printed in Europe, USA, Canada, Australia, Japan

Cover: Foto ©ninafisch / pixelio.de

More available books at **www.hansebooks.com**

CATALOGUE

OF

New and Practical.

BOOKS.

LONDON:

L. UPCOTT GILL, "THE BAZAAR" OFFICE, 170, STRAND.

No. 3*.—1881.

Of Englishe Dogges,
the diuersities, the names,
the natures, and the properties.

A Short
Treatise written in latine
by Iohannes Caius of late memorie, Doctor of Phisicke
in the Vniuersitie
of Cambridge,

And newly drawne into Englishe by Abraham Fle-
ming Student.

Natura etiam in brutis viro
oStendit suam.

Seene and allowed.

¶ Imprinted at London
by Rychard Iohnes, and are to be
solde ouer againſt S. Sepulchres Church without
Newgate.
1576.

¶ A Profopopoicall fpeache
of the Booke.

SOme tell of starres th'influence straunge,
  Some tell of byrdes which flie in th'ayre,
Some tell of beastes on land which raunge.
  Some tell of fishe in riuers fayre,
Some tell of serpentes sundry sortes,
  Some tell of plantes the full effect,
Of English dogges I sound reportes,
  Their names and natures I detect,
My forhed is but baulde and bare :
  But yet my bod'ys beutifull,
For pleasaunt flowres in me there are,
  And not so fyne as plentifull :
And though my garden plot so greene.
  Of dogges receaue the trampling feete,
Yet is it swept and kept full cleene,
  So that it yeelds a sauour sweete.

.Ih.Fle.

DOCTISSIMO VIRO, ET

Patrono ſuo ſingulari D. Perne, E-
lienſis eccleſiæ Cathedralis digniſsi-
mo Decano, Abrahamus Flemingus,

ιυδαιμονιαν.

Cripſit non multis abhinc annis (op-
time Patrone) et non impolitè scripsit, vir
omnibus optimarum literarum remis instruc-
tissimus, de doctorum grege non malè meritus,
tuæ dignitati familiaritatis nexu coniunctissi-
mus, clarissimum Cantabrigiensis academiæ
lumen, gēma, et gloria, Johannes Caius, ad
Conradum Gesnerum summum suum, hominem peritissimum, indaga-
torem rerum reconditarum sagacissimum, pulcherrimaq. historiarum
naturalium panoplia exornatü, epitomen de cambus Britannicis non
tam breuem quàm elegantem, et vtilem, epitomen inquam variis
variorum experimentorum argumentis concinnatam; in cuius titulum
cū forte incidissem, et nouitate re inonnihil delectarer, interpretationem
Anglicam aggressus sum. Postquam vero finem penso imposuissem,
repentina quædam de opusculi dedicatione cogitatio oboriebatur tādemque
post multas multarum rerum iactationes, beneficiarum tuorum (Orna-
tīssime vir) vnica recordatio, instar rutilantis stellæ, qnæ radiorum
splendore quaslibet caliginosas teterrimæ obliuionis nebulas dissipat,
et memoriæ serenitatem, plusquā solarem, inducit, mihi illuxit; nec nō
officii ratio quæ funestissimis insensæ fortunæ fulminibus conquassata,
lacerata, et convulsa, penè perierat, fractas vires multumq. debilitatas
colligebat, pristinum robur recuperauit, tandemque aliquando ex Lethea
illa palude neruose emergebat, atque eluctata est. Quā voraginē
simulatque euaserat, sic effloruit, adeoque increuit, vt vnamquamque

animi mei cellulã in sui ditionem atque imperii amplitudinem raperet. Nunc vero in contemplatione meritorum tuorum versari non desino, quorum magnitudinem nescio an tam tenui et leuidensi orationis filo possim circumscribere : Hoc, Ædepol, me non mediocriter monet, non leuiter torquet, non languide pungit. Est præterea alia causa quæ mihi scrupulum injicit, et quodammodo exulcerat, ingrati nempe animi suspicio a qua, tanquam ab aliqua Lernæa Hydra, pedibus (vt aiunt) Achilleis semper fugi, et tamē valde pertimesco ne officij mora et procrastinatio (vt ita dicam) obscœnam securitatis labem nomini meo inurat, eoque magis expauesco quod peruulgatum illud atque decantatum poetæ carmen memoriæ occurrebat.

Dedecus est semper sumere nilque dare.

Sed (Ornatissime vir) quemadmodū metus illius mali me magnopere affligebat atque fodicabat, ita spes alterius boni, nempe humanitatis tuæ, qua cæteris multis interuallis præluxeris, origit suffulcitque : Ea etiam spes alma et opima iubet et hortatur aliquod quale qualo sit, officij specimen cum allacritate animi prodere. Hisce itaque persuasionibus victus me morigerum præbui, absolutamque de canibus Britannicis interpretationē Anglicam, tibi potissimum vtpote patrono singulari, et vnico Mœcenati dedicandū proposui : non quod tam ieiuno et exili munere immensum meritorum tuorum mare metiri machiner, non quod religiosas aures sacratasque, prophanæ paginæ explicatione obtundere cupiam, nec quod nugatoriis friuolisque narrationibus te delectari arbitrer, cum in diuinioribus exercitationibus totus sis : sed potius (cedat fides dicto) quod insignis ille egregiusque liber alium artium, et præcipuè medicæ facultatis princeps (qui hoc opusculum contexuit) ita viguit dum vixerat adeoque inclaruit, vt haud scio (vt ingenué fatear quod sentio) an post funer a parem sibi superstitem reliquerit. Deinde quod hunc libellum summo studio et industria elaboratum in transmarinas regiones miserat, ad hominem omni literarum genere, et præsertim occultarū rerum

Dedicatoria.

cognitione, quæ intimis naturæ visceribus et medullis insederat (O in-
geniū niueo lapillo dignū) cuius difficultates Laberyntheis anfractibus
flexuosisque recessibus impeditas perscrutari et inuestigare (deus bone,
quam ingēs labor, quam infinitum opus,) excultum, Conradum Gesnerum
scriberet, quæ tantam gratiam conciliauit vt non solum amicissimo osculo
exciperet, sed etiam studiose lectitaret, accuratè vteretur, inexhaustis
denique viribus, tanquam perspicacissimus draco vellus aureum, et oculis
plusquam aquilinis custodiret.   Postremo quemadmodum hanc epitomen
à viro verè docto ad virum summa nominis celebritate decoratum scriptam
fuisse accepimus, ita eandem ipsam (pro titulo Britānnico) Britanico
sermone, licet ineleganti, vsitata et populari, ab esuriente Rhetore
donatam, tuis (eruditissime vir) manibus commendo vt tuo sub patrocino
in has atque illas regionis nostræ partes intrepide proficiscatur; obtes-
torque ut hunc libellum, humilem et obscuram inscriptionem
gerentem, argumentum nouum et antehæc non auditum
complectientem, ab omni tamen Sybaritica
obscœnitate remotissimum,   æqui
bonique consulas,

Tue dignitati deditifsimus

Abrahamus

Flemingus.

Translation.

To the most learned man, and his especial patron, E. Perne,
most worthy Dean of Ely Cathedral church, Abraham
Fleming dedicates.

Not many years ago (O best of patrons) a man most advised in every branch of life; one who has deserved well of the company of the learned; bound by the ties of family to yourself; a most shining light of the University of Cambridge; its jewel and glory, John Caius, wrote not without elegance to Conrad Gesner, a man exceedingly skilled and sagacious in the investigation of recondite matters; a man armed with everything that relates to natural history; the same man wrote an epitome concerning British dogs, not so concise as elegant and useful; an epitome compact of the various arguments and experiences of many minds; a book which when by chance I had met with it, and was covered with delight with the novelty of its appearance, I attempted to translate into English. After I had finished my task, a sudden conceit arose in me touching the dedication of the pamphlet, and after tossing many thoughts to and fro, the recollections (most ornate sir) of your benefits, as a ruddy star, by the splendour of its radiance, dissipates the misty clouds of the most foul oblivion, and brings a serenity brighter than that of the sun to the memory, shone on me; and that sentiment of duty which shaken by the most deadly bolts of hostile fortune torn and convulsed, had almost died, collected its shattered and most weakened strength, recovered its pristine vigour, and at last, from that bog of Lethe, nobly extricated itself and emerged. Out of which whirlpool as soon as it had escaped, it so flourished and so increased that it caught every cell of my mind under the influence of its rule and command. Now, however, I cease not to be occupied in the contemplation of your merits, the magnitude of which can scarcely be circumscribed in my thin coarse and slight thread of speech. This fact, by Jove, does not move me lightly, distresses me in no common manner, and pricks me with no shallow wound. There is besides another cause, which makes me pause, and in some manner tortures me, namely the suspicion of ingratitude, from which, as from another Lernean hydra, I have ever fled (as the phrase runs) with Achillean feet, and still I very much fear lest delay and procrastination of my duty brand my name with a shameful mark of carelessness. This so much the more I fear because that truth and common verse of the poet comes into my mind

It is a shame always to receive and never to give.

But (O most ornate Sir!) however the fear of that ill mightily stirs and

Translation (continued).

discomposes me, yet the expectation of another good, that is of your humanity, in which quality you shine far beyond other men, restores and buoys me up. That gentle and excellent hope commands and exhorts me to produce some specimen or token of my duty, however small, with alacrity. By these inducements conquered, I proposed free interpretation into English of the treatise on British dogs, and have dedicated it to you rather than to anyone else as my one patron, and unique Mæcenas. Not because I supposed that the unmeasurable sea of your merits could be gaged by so jejune and poor a gift; not because I was anxious to weary your sacred and religious years with the explanation of a profane page ; nor because I supposed that you would be delighted with idle and frivolous matter, occupied as you are entirely in divine lucubrations, but rather (if I may be believed) because that egregious and noble prince of the liberal arts, and more especially of the faculty of medicine, who composed this work, so flourished while he lived, and obtained so brilliant a fame, that I know not honestly to confess what I feel, if after his death, he has left any like him. Lastly because he had sent this little book to Conrad Gesner, elaborated with the utmost industry into lands beyond the sea, to a man remarkable for his knowledge of all kinds of literature, and especially for his acquaintance with occult matters, which is settled in the inmost bowels and marrows of Nature (O talent worthy of a white stone !), whose difficulties, entangled by Labyrinthian windings and tortuous flexuosities I have investigated (O good God ! how great a labour and how infinite a travail !) which raised such favour and conciliation in the breast of Conrad Gesner, that he not only received it with a friendly kiss, but also read it studiously, and used it accurately, with the inexhausted strength by which the dragon guards the fleece of gold, and kept it with more vigilant eyes than the eagle. Lastly, since we have heard that this epitome was written by a truly learned man to a man adorned with the highest celebrity of fame, so the epitome, in English speech, however inelegant, is yet common and popular to your hands. O most erudite Sir, I beseech you to command, that under your patronage, it may boldly go forth into all parts of our country, and I solemnly pray you to receive from me this book bearing a humble and obscure inscription, but embracing an argument new and as yet unheard of ; as well as entirely free from any Sybaritic obscenity.

The most bounden to your service,

(Signed)   ABRAHAM FLEMING.

To the well difpofed Reader.

S euery manifeſt effect procceedeth frõ som certain cause, so the penning of this present abridgement (gentle and courteous reader) issued from a speciall occasion. For Conradus Gesnerus, a mań whiles he liued, of incomparable knowledge, and manyfold experience, being neuer satisfied with the sweete sappe of vnderstanding, reqnested *Iohannes Caius* a profound clarke and a rauennous deuourer of learning (to his praise be it spokē, though the language be somewhat homely) to write a breuiary or short treatise of such dogges as were ingendred within the borders of England : To the contentation of whose minde and the vtter accomplishcment of whose desire, *Caius* spared no study, (for the acquaintance which was betweene them, as it was confirmed by continuaunce, and established vpon vnfainednes, so was it sealed with vertue and honesty), withdrew himself from no labour, repined at no paines, forsooke no trauaile, refused no endeuour, finally pretermitted no opportunity or circnmstaunce which seemed pertinent and requisite to the performance of this litle libell. In the whole discourse wherof, the booke, to consider the substaunce, being but a pamphlet or skantling, the argument not so fyne and affected, and yet the doctrine very profitable and necessarye, he vseth such a smoothe and comely style, and tyeth his inuention to such methodicall and orderly proceedings, as the elegantnes and neatnesse of his Latine phrase (being pure, perfeet, and vnmingled) maketh the matter which of it selfe is very base and clubbishe, to appeare (shall I say tollerable) nay rather commendable and effectuall. The sundry sortes of

Englishe dogges he discouereth so euidently, their natures he rippeth vp so apparently, their manners he openeth so manifestly, their qualities he declareth so skilfully, their proportions he painteth out so perfectly, their colours he describeth so artificially, and knytteth all these in such shortnesse and breuity, that the mouth of th'adversary must needes confesse & giue sentence that commendation ought to bee his rewarde, and praise his deserued pension. An ignoraunt man woulde neuer have beene drawne into this opinion, to thincke that there had bene in England such variety & choice of dogges, in all respectes (not onely for name but also for qualitie) so diuerso and vnlike. But what cannot learning attaine? what cannot the kay of knowledge open? what cannot the lampe of vnderstanding lighten? what secretes cannot discretion detect? finally what cannot experience comprehend? what huge heapes of histories hath *Gesnerus* hourded vp in volumes of a large syze? Fishes in floudes, Cattell on lande, Byrdes in the ayre, how hath he sifted them by their naturall differences, how closely and in how narrow a compasse hath he couched mighty and monstruous beasts, in bygnesse lyke mountaines, the bookes themselues being lesser then Molehilles. The lyfe of this man was not so great a restrority of comfort, as his death was an vlcer or wound of sorrow; the losse of whom *Caius* lamented, not so much as he was his faithfull friende, as for that he was a famous Philosupher, and yet the former reason (being in very deede vehement and forceable) did stinge him with more griefe, then he peraduenture was willing to disclose. And though death be counted terrible for the time, and consequently vnhappy, yet *Caius* aduoucheth the death of *Gesner* most blessed, luckie, and fortunate, as in his Booke intituled *De libris propijs*, appeareth. But of these two Eagles sufficient is spoken as I suppose, and yet litle enough in consideration of their dignitie and worthines. Neurthelesse litle or mickle, something or nothing, substaunce or shadow take all in good part, my meaning is by a

To the Reader.

fewe wordes to wynne credit to this worke, not so much for mine owne Englishe Translation as for the singular commendation of them, challenged of dutie and desart. Wherefore gentle Reader I commit them to thy memorie, and their bookes to thy courteous censure. They were both learned men, and painefull practitioners in their professions, so much the more therfore are their workes worthy estimation, I would it were in me to advaunce them as I wishe, the worst (and yet both, no doubt, excellent) hath deserued a monument of immortality. Well there is no more to be added but this, that as the translatiō of this booke was attempted, finished, and published of goodwill (not onely to administer pleasure, as to affoord profit) so it is my desire and request that my labour therin employed may be acceptable, as I hope it shalbe to men of indifferent iudgement. As for such as shall snarr and suatch at the Englishe abrydgement, and te are the Translatour, being absent, with the teeth of spightfull enuye, I conclude in breuity there eloquence is but currishe, if I serue in their meat with wrong sawce, ascribe it not to vnskilfulnesse in coquery, but to ignoraunce in their diet, for as the Poet sayeth

> *Non satis est ars sola coquo, scuire palato :*
> *Nanque coquus domini debet habere gulam ;*

> It is not enough that a cooke vnderstand,
> Except his Lordes stomack he holde in his hand.

To winde vp all in a watcheworde I saye no more, But doe well, and Farewell.

His and his Friendes,
Abraham
Fleming.

The firſt Section of this
diſcourſe.

*Wrote unto you (well beloued friend
Geſner) not many yeares past, a manyfolde his-
torie, contayning the diuers formes and figures
of Beastes, Byrdes, and Fyshes, the sundry
shapes of plantes, and the fashions of Hearbes,
&c.*

I wrote moreouer, vnto you seuerally, a cer-
taine abridgement of Dogges, which in your discourse vpon the fourmes
of Beastes in the seconde order of mylde and tameable Beastes,
where you make mencion of Scottishe Dogges, and in the wynding vp
of your Letter written and directed to Doctour *Turner*, comprehending
a Catalogue or rehersall of your bookes not yet extant, you promised
to set forth in print, and openly to publishe in the face of the worlde
among such your workes as are not yet come abroade to lyght and
sight. But, because certaine circumstaunces were wanting in my
breuary of Englishe Dogges (as seemed vnto mee), I stayed the publi-
cation of the same, making promise to send another abroade, which
myght be commytted to the handes, the eyes, the eares, the mindes,
and the iudgements of the Readers. Wherefore that I myght perfourme
that preciselye which I promised solempnly, accomplishe my deter-
mination, and satisfy your expectacion: which art a man desirous

and capeable of all kinde of knowledge, and very earnest to be acquainted with all experimentes : I wyll expresse and declare in due order, the grand and generall kinde of English Dogges, the difference of them, the vse, the propertyes and the diuerse natures of the same, making a tripartite diuision in this sort and maner.

All English Dogges be eyther of,
$$\begin{cases} \text{A gentle kinde, seruing the game.} \\ \text{A homely kind, apt for sundry necessary vses.} \\ \text{A currishe kinde, meete for many toyes.} \end{cases}$$

Of these three sortes or kindes so meane I to entreate, that the first in the first place, the last in the last roome, and the myddle sort in the middle seate be handled. I cal the vniuersally all by the name of Englishe dogges, as well because England only, as it hath in it English dogs, so it is not without Scottishe, as also for that wee are more inclined and delighted with the noble game of hunting, for we Englishmen are adicted and giuen to that exercise, and painefull pastime of pleasure, as well for the plenty of fleshe which our Parkes and Forests doe foster, as also for the opertunitie and connenient leisure which wee obtaine, both which, the Scottes want. Wherefore seeing that the whole estate of kindly hunting consisteth principally,

In these two pointes,
$$\begin{cases} \text{In chasing the beast} \\ \text{In taking the byrde} \end{cases} \text{that} \begin{cases} \text{hunting} \\ \text{is in} \end{cases} \begin{cases} \text{hunting} \\ \text{fowleing} \end{cases}$$

It is necessary and requisite to vnderstand, that there are two sortes of Dogges by whose meanes, the feates within specifyed are wrought, and these practyces of actinetie cunningly and curiously compassed.

Two kindes of Dogges
$$\begin{cases} \text{One which rouseth the beast and continueth the chase.} \\ \text{Another which spryngeth the byrde and bewrayeth flight by pursuite,} \end{cases}$$

Englifhe Dogges.

33

Both which kyndes are tearmed of the Latines by one common name
that is, *Canes Venatici*, hunting dogges. But because we Englifhe men
make a difference betweene hunting and fowleing, for that they are
called by these seurall wordes, *Venatio & Aucupium*, so they tearme
the Dogges whom they vse in these sundry games by diuers names, as
those which serue for the beast, are called *Venatici*, the other which are
vsed for the fowle are called *Aucupatorij*.

The first kind
called *Venatici*
I diuide into
fiue sorts.

> The first in perfect smelling
> The second in quicke spying
> The thirde in swiftnesse and quicknesse
> The fourth in smeling & nymblenesse
> The fifte in subtiltie and deceitfulnesse,

Excelleth.

Of the Dogge called a Harrier, in
Latine *Leuerarius*.

THat kinde of dogge whom nature hath indued with the vertue of
smelling, whose property it is to vse a lustines, a readines,
and a courageousnes in hunting, and draweth into his nostrells the
ayre or sent of the beast pursued and followed, we call by this word
Sagax, the *Grecians* by thys word ιχνιυτιυ of tracing or chasing by ẏ
foote, or ſỉυυλάτιυ of the nostrells, which be the instrumentes of
smelling. Wee may knowe these kinde of Dogges by their long,
large, and bagging lippes, by their hanging eares, reachyng downe
both sydes of their chappes, and by the indifferent and measurable
proportion of their making. This sort of Dogges we call *Leuararios*
Hariers, that I may comprise the whole nūber of them in certaine
specialties, and apply to them their proper and peculier names, for
so much as they cannot all be reduced and brought vnder one

sorte, considering both the sundrye uses of them, and the difference of their seruice whereto they be appointed.

Some for	The Hare The Foxe The Wolfe The Harte The Bucke The Badger The Otter The Polcat The Lobster The Weasell The Conny, &c.	Some for one thing and some for another.

As for the Conny, whom we haue lastly set downe, wee use not to hunt, but rather to take it, somtime with the nette sometime with the ferret, and thus euery seuerall sort is notable and excellent in his naturall qualitie and appointed practice. Among these sundry sortes, there be some which are apt to hunt two diuers beastes, as the Foxe otherwhiles, and other whiles the Hare, but they hunt not with such towardnes and good lucke after them, as they doe that whereunto nature hath formed and framed them, not onely in externall composition & making, but also inward faculties and conditions, for they swarue sometimes, and doo otherwise then they should.

Of the Dogge called Terrar, in Latine *Terrarius*.

A Nother sorte there is which hunteth the Foxe and the Badger or Greye onely, whom we call Terrars, because they (after the manner and custome of ferrets in searching for Connyes) creepe into the grounde, and by that meanes make afrayde, nyppe, and byte the Foxe and the

Badger in such sort, that eyther they teare them in pieces with theyr
teeth beyng in the bosome of the earth, or else hayle and pull them
perforce out of their lurking angles, darke dongeons, and close caues, or
at the least through cöcened feare, driue them out of their hollow har-
bours, in so much that they are compelled to prepare speedy flight, and
being desirous of the next (albeit not the safest) refuge, are otherwise
taken and intrapped with snares and nettes layde ouer holes to the same
purpose. But these be the least in that kynde called *Sagax*.

Of the Dogge called a Bloudhounde in
Latine *Sanguinarius*.

THe greater sort which serue to hunt, hauing lippes of a large syze
& eares of no small lenght, doo, not onely chase the beast whiles
it liueth (as the other doo of whom mencion aboue is made) but beyng
dead also by any maner of casualtie, make recourse to the place where it
lyeth, hauing in this poynt an assured and infallible guyde, namely, the
sent and sauour of the bloud sprinckled heere and there vpon the ground.
For whether the beast beyng wounded, doth notwithstanding enioye life,
and escapeth the handes of the huntesman, or whether the said beast
beyng slayne is conuayed clenly out of the parcke (so that there be
some signification of bloud shed) these Dogges with no lesse facilitie
and easinesse, then auiditie and greedinesse, can disclose and bewray the
same by smelling, applying to their pursuit, agilitie and nimblenesse, without tediousnesse, for which consideration, of a singuler specialitie they
deserued to bee called *Sanguinarij* bloudhounds. And albeit peraduenture it may chaunce, (As whether it chaunceth sealdome or sometime I am
ignorant) that a pecce of fleshe be subtily stolne and conningly conuayed
away with such prouisos and precaueats as thereby all apparaunce of
bloud is eyther preuented, excluded, or concealed, yet these kinde of

dogges by a certaine direcion of an inwarde assured notyce and priuy
marcke, pursue the deede dooers, through long lanes, crooked reaches,
and weary wayes, without wandring awry out of the limites of the land
whereon those desperate purloyners prepared their speedy passage. Yea,
the natures of these Dogges is such, and so effectuall is their foresight,
that they cā bewray, seperate, and pycke them out from among an infinite multitude and an innumerable company, creepe they neuer so
farre into the thickest thronge, they will finde him out notwithstandyng he lye hidden in wylde woods, in close and ouergrowen
groues, and lurcke in hollow holes apte to harbour such vngracious
guestes. Moreouer, although they should passe ouer the water, thinking
thereby to auoyde the pursute of the houndes, yet will not these dogges
giue ouer their attempt, but presuming to swym through the streame,
perseuer in their pursute, and when they be arriued and gotten the
furthen bancke, they hunt vp and downe, to and fro runne they, from
place to place shift they, vntil they haue attained to that plot of
grounde where they passed ouer. And this is their practise, if perdie
they cānot at y' first time smelling, finde out the way which the deede
dooers tooke to escape. So at length get they that by arte, cunning,
and dilligent indeuour, which by fortune and lucke they cannot otherwyse
ouercome. In so much that it seemeth worthely and wisely written by
Ælianus in his firte book and xxxiv. Chapter. Τὸιυέυμντιχον χαιδιαι ινχτιχ.
to bee as it were naturally instilled and powered into these kinde of
dogges. For they wyll not pause or breath from their pursute vntill such
tyme as they bee apprehended and taken that committed the facte. The
owners of such houndes vse to keepe them in close and darke channells
in the day time, and let them lose at liberty in the night season, to
th'intent that they myght with more courage and boldnesse practise
to follow the fellon in the euening and solitarie houres of darkenesse,
when such yll disposed varlots are principally purposed to play theyr

impudent pageants, and imprudent pranckes. These houndes (vpon whom this present portion of our treatise runneth) when they are to follow such fellowes as we haue before rehersed, vse not that liberty to raunge at wil, which they have otherwise when they are in game (except vpon necessary occasion, whereon dependeth an urgent an effectuall perswasion), when such purloyners make spædy way in flight, but beyng restrained and drawne backe from running at random with the leasse, the ende whereof the owner holding in his hand is led, guyded and directed with such swiftenesse and slownesse (whether he go on foote or whether he ryde on horsebacke), as he himselfe in harte would wishe for the more easie apprehension of these venturous varlots. In the borders of England and Scotland (the often and accustomed stealing of cattell so procuring) these kinde of Dogges are very much vsed and they are taught and trayned up first of all to hunt cattell as well of the smaller as of the greater grouth, and afterwardes (that qualitie relinquished and lefte) they are learned to pursue such pestilent persons as plant theyr pleasure in such practises of purloyning as we have already declared. Of this kinde there is nene that taketh the water naturally, except it please you so to suppose of them whych follow the Otter, whych sometimes haunte the lande, and sometime useth the water. And yet neuerthelesse all the kind of them boyling and boyling with greedy desire of the pray which by swymming passeth through riuer and flood, plung amyds the water, and passe the streame with their pawes. But this propertie proceedeth from an earnest desire wherwith they be inflamed, rather then from any inclination issuyng from the ordinance and appoyntment of nature. And albeit some of this sort in English be called *Brache*, in Scottishe *Rache*, the cause hereof resteth in the shee sex and not in the generall kinde, for we English men call bytches belonging to the hunting kinde of Dogges, by the tearme aboue mencioned. To bee short it is proper to the nature of houndes, some to keepe silence in hunting untill

C

such tyme as there is game offered.   Other some so soone as they smell
out the place where the beast lurcketh, to bewray it immediately by
their importunate barcking, notwithstanding it be farre of many furlongs
cowchyng close in his cabbyn.   And these Dogges the younger they
be, the more wantonly barcke they, and the more liberally, yet
oftimes without necessitie, so that in them, by reason of theyr young
yeares and want of practise, small certaintie is to be reposed.   For con-
tinuance of tyme, and experience in game, ministreth to these houndes
not onely cunning in running, but also (as in the rest) an assured foresight what is to bee done, principally, being acquainted with their
masters watchwordes, eyther in reuoking or imboldening them to scrue
the game.

Of the Dogge called the Gaschounde, in
Latine *Agaseus.*

THis kinde of Dogge which pursueth by the eye, preuayleth little, or
neuer a whit, by any benefite of the nose that is by smelling, but
excelleth in perspicuitie and sharpenesse of sight altogether, by the
vertue whereof, being singuler and notable, it hunteth the Foxe and the
Hare.   Thys Dogge will choose and seperate any beast from among
a great flocke or hearde, and such a one will it take by election as is
not lancke, leane and hollow, but well spyed, smoothe, full, fatte,
and round, it followes by the direction of the eyesight, which in deede
is cleere constant, and not uncertaine, if a beast be wounded and gone
astray this Dogge seeketh after it by the steadfastnes of the eye, if it
chaunce peraduenture to returne and be mingled with the residue of the
flocke, this Dogge spyeth it out by the vertue of his eye, leauing the
rest of the cattell vntouched, and after he hath set sure sight upō
it, he seperateth it from among the company and hauing so done neuer

ceaseth untill he haue wearyed the Beast to death. Our countrey
men call this dogge *Ayasœum.* A gasehounde because the beames
of his sight are so stedfastly setled and vnmoueably fastened. These
Dogges are much and vsually occupyed in the Northern partes of England more then in the Southern parts, and in fealdy landes rather then
in bushy and wooddy places, horsemen vse them more then footemen to
th'intent that they might prouoke their horses to a swift galloppe (wherwith they are more delighted then with the pray it selfe), and that they
might accustome theyr horse to leape ouer hedges and ditches, without
stoppe or stumble, without harme or hassard, without doubt or daunger,
and so escape with safegard of lyfe. And to the ende that the ryders
themselues when necessitie so constrained, and the feare of further mischiefe inforced, myght saue themselues vndamnifyed, and preuent each
perilous tempest by preparing speedy flight, or else by swift pursute made
vpon theyr enimyes, myght both ouertake them, encounter with them,
and make a slaughter of them accordingly. But if it fortune so at any
time that this Dogge take a wrong way, the master making some vsual
signe and familiar token, he returneth forthwith, and taketh the right
and ready trace, beginning his chase a fresh, & with a cleare voyce, and
a swift foote followeth the game with as much courage and nimblenesse
as he did at the first.

Of the Dogge called the Grehounde, in
Latine *Leporarius.*

THere is another kinde of Dogge which for his incredible swiftnesse
is called *Leporarius* a Grehounde because the principall seruice of
them dependeth and consisteth in starting and hunting the hare, which
Dogges likewyse are indued with no lesse strength then lightnes in main-
tenance of the game, in seruing the chase, in taking the Bucke, the

c 2

Harte, the Dowe, the Foxe, and other beastes of semblable kinde ordained for the game of hunting. But more or lesse, each one according to the measure and proportion of theyr desire, and as might and habilitie of theyr bodyes will permit and suffer. For it is a spare and bare kinde of Dogge, (of fleshe but not of bone) some are of a greater sorte, and some of a lesser, some are smooth skynned & some are curled, the bigger therefore are appoynted to hunt the bigger beasts, & the smaller serue to hunt the smaller accordingly. The nature of these dogges I find to be wonderful by y' testimoniall of histories. For, as John Froisart the Historiographer in his 4. lib. reporteth. A Grehound of King Richard, the second y' wore the Crowne and bare the Scepter of the Realme of England, neuer knowing any man, beside the Kings person, whō *Henry Duke* of *Lancaster* came to the castle of *Flinte* to take King *Richarde.* The Dogge forsaking his former Lord & master came to *Duke Henry,* fawned upon him with such resemblaunces of goodwyll and conceaued affection, as he fauoured King *Richarde* before: he followed the Duke, and vtterly left the King. So that by these manifest circumstances a man myght iudge this Dogge to haue bene lightened wyth the lampe of foreknowledge & vnderstāding, touch-yng his olde masters miseryes to come, and vnhappinesse nye at hand, which King *Richarde* himselfe cuidently perceaued, accounting this deede of his Dogge a Prophecy of his ouerthrowe.

Of the Dogge called the Leuiner, or Lyemmer
in Latine *Lorarius.*

Another sort of dogges be there, in smelling singuler, and in swiftenesse incomparable. This is (as it were) a myddle kinde betwixt the Harier and the Grehounde, as well for his kinde, as for the frame of his body. And it is called in latine *Leuinarius, a Leuitate,* of lyghtnesse, and therefore may well be called a lyght hounde, it is also called by this worde *Lorarius, a Loro*, wherewith it is led. This Dogge for the excellency of his conditions, namely smelling and swift running, doth followe the game with more eagernes, and taketh the pray with a iolly quicknes.

Of the Dogge called a Tumbler, in Latine *Vertagus*.

THis sorte of Dogges, which compasseth all by craftes, fraudes, subtelties and deceiptes, we Englishe men call Tvmblers, because in hunting they turne and tumble, winding their bodyes about in circle wise, and then fearcely and violently venturing upõ the beast, doth soddenly gripe it, at the very entrance and mouth of their receptacles, or closets before they can recouer meanes, to saue and succour themselves. This dogge vseth another craft and subteltie, namely, when he runneth into a warren, or setteth a course about a connyburrough, he huntes not after them, he frayes them not by barcking, he makes no countenance or shadow of hatred against them, but dissembling friendship, and pretend-ing fauour, passeth by with silence and quietnesse, marking and noting their holes diligently, wherin (I warrant you) he will not be ouershot nor deceaued. When he commeth to the place where Connyes be, of a certaintie, he cowcheth downe close with his belly to the groũd, Pro-vided alwayes by his skill and polisie, that y' the winde bee neuer with him but against him in such an enterprise. And that the Connyes spie him not where he lurcketh. By which meanes he obtaineth the sent and sauour of the Connyes, carryed towardes him with the wind & the ayre, either going to their holes, or cõming out, eyther passing this way, or running that way, and so prouideth by his circumspection, that the selly simple Conny is debarred quite from his hole (which is the hauen

of their hope and the harbour of their health) and fraudulently circum-
uented and taken, before they can get the aduantage of their hole. Thus
hauing caught his pray he carryeth it speedily to his Master, wayting
his Dogges returne in some conuenient lurcking corner. These Dogges
are somewhat lesser than the houndes, and they be lancker & leaner,
beside that they be somwhat prick eared. A man that shall marke the
forme and fashion of their bodyes, may well call them mungrell
Grehoundes if they were somwhat bigger. But notwithstanding they
counteruaile not the Grehound in greatnes, yet will he take in one
dayes space as many Connyes as shall arise to as bigge a burthen, and as
heauy a loade as a horse can carry, for deceipt and guile is the instrument wherby he maketh this spoyle, which pernicious properties supply
the places of more commendable qualities.

Of the Dogge called the theeuishe Dogge
in Latine *Canis furax*.

THe like to that whom we haue rehearsed, is the theeuishe Dogge,
which at the mandate and bydding of his master steereth and
leereth abroade in the night, hunting Connyes by the ayre, which is
leuened with their sauer and conueyed to the sense of smelling by the
meanes of the winde blowing towardes him. During all which space of
his hunting he will not barcke, least he shoulde bee preuidiciall to his
owne aduantage. And thus watcheth and snatcheth up in course as
many Connyes as his Master will suffer him, and beareth them to his
Masters standing. The farmers of the countrey and uplandishe dwellers,
call this kinde of Dogge a nyght curre, because he hunteth in the darke,
But let thus much seeme sufficient for Dogges which serue the game, and
disport of hunting.

¶ A Diall pertaining to the
firft Section.

| Dogges seruing y' pastime of hunting beastes. | are diuided into | Hariers
Terrars
Bloudhounds
Gasehounds
Grehounds
Leuiners or
Lyemmers
Tumblers
Stealers | In Latine called *Ve-natici.* |

The feconde Section of
this difcourfe.

Of gentle Dogges feruing the hauke, and first
of the Spaniell, called in Latine
Hifpaniolus.

Vch Dogges as ferue for fowling, I
thinke conuenient and requisite to place in this
seconde Section of this treatise. These are also
to bee reckoned and accounted in the number
of the dogges which come of a gentle kind, and
of those which serue for fowling.

		The first findeth game on the land.
There be two sortes		
		The other findeth game on the water.

Such as delight on the land, play their partes, eyther by swiftnesse of
foote, or by often questing, to search out and to spying the byrde for
further hope of aduauntage, or else by some secrete signe and priuy token
bewray the place where they fall.

The first kinde of such serue	The Hauke,
The seconde,	The net, or, traine,

The first kinde haue no peculier names assigned vnto them, sane
onely that they be denominated after the byrde which by naturall

appointment he is alotted to take, for the which consideration.

Some be called Dogges, { For the Falcon / The Phesant / The Partridge } and such like,

The common sort of people call them by one generall word, namely Spaniells. As though these kinde of Dogges came originally and first of all out of Spaine, The most part of their skynnes are white, and if they be marcked with any spottes, they are commonly red, and somewhat great therewithall, the heares not growing in such thicknesse but that the mixture of them maye easely be perceaued. Othersome of them be reddishe and blackishe, but of that sorte there be but a very few. There is also at this day among vs a newe kinde of dogge brought out of Fraunce (for we Englishe men are maruailous greedy gaping gluttons after nouelties, and couetous cornorauntes of things that be seldom, rare, straunge, and hard to get.) And they bee speckled all ouer with white and black, which mingled colours incline to a marble blewe, which bewtifyeth their skinnes and affordeth a seemely show of comlynesse. These are called French dogges as is aboue declared already.

The Dogge called the Setter, in Latine *Index.*

ANother sort of Dogges be there, scruiceable for fowling, making no noise either with foote or with tounge, whiles they followe the game. These attend diligently vpon theyr Master and frame their conditions to such beckes, motions, and gestures, as it shall please him to exhibite and make, either going forward, drawing backeward, inclining to the right hand, or yealding toward the left, (In making mencion of fowles my meaning is of the Partridge and the Quaile) when he hath founde the byrde, he keepeth sure and fast silence, he stayeth his steppes and wil proceede no further, and with a

close, couert, watching eye, layeth his belly to the grounde and
so creepeth forward like a worme.   When he approcheth neere to
the place where the birde is, he layes him downe, and with a marcke
of his pawes, betrayeth the place of the byrdes last abode, whereby
it is supposed that this kinde of dogge is called *Index*, Setter, being
in deede a name most consonant and agreable to his quality.   The
place being knowne by the meanes of the dogge, the fowler immediatly
openeth and spreedeth his net, intending to take them, which being done
the dogge at the accustomed becke or vsuall signe of his Master ryseth
vp by and by, and draweth neerer to the fowle that by his presence they
might be the authors of their owne insnaring, and be ready intangled in
the prepared net, which conning and artificiall indeuour in a dogge
(being a creature domesticall or householde seruaunt brought vp at home
with offalls of the trencher and fragments of victualls) is not much to be
maruailed at, seing that a Hare (being a wilde and skippishe beast) was
seene in England to the astonishment of the beholders, in the yeare of our
Lorde God, 1564 not onely daunciyng in measure, but playing with his
former feete vppon a tabbaret, and obseruing iust number of strokes (as
a practicioner in that arte) besides that nipping & pinching a dogge
with his teeth and clawes, & cruelly thumping him with y' force of his
feete.   This is no trumpery tale, nor trifling toye (as I imagine) and
therefore not vnworthy to be reported, for I recken it a requitall of my
trauaile, not to drowne in the seas of silence any speciall thing, wherein
the prouidence and effectuall working of nature is to be pondered.

Of the Dogge called the water Spaniell, or finder,

in Latine *Aquaticus seuinquisitor.*

THat kinde of dogge whose seruice is required in fowling vpon the
water, partly through a naturall towardnesse, and partly by

diligent teaching, is indued with that property. This sort is somewhat bigge, and of a measurable greatnesse, hauing long, rough, and curled heare, not obtayned by extraordinary trades, but giuen by natures appointment, yet neuerthelesse (friend *Gesner*) I haue described and set him out in this maner, namely powlde and notted from the shoulders to the hindermost legges, and to the end of his tayle, which I did for use and customs cause, that beyng as it were made somewhat bare and naked, by shearing of such superfluitie of heare, they might atchiue the more lightnesse, and swiftnesse, and be lesse hindered in swymming, so troublesome and needelesse a burthen being shaken of. This kinde of dogge is properly called *Aquaticus*, a water spaniel because he frequenteth and hath vsual recourse to the water where all his game & exercise lyeth, namely, waterfowles, which are taken by the helpe & seruice of them, in their kind. And principally duckes and drakes, wherupon he is lykewise named a dogge for the ducke, because in that qualitie he is excellent. With these dogges also we fetche out of the water such fowle as be stounge to death by any venemous worme, we vse them also to bring vs our boultes & arrowes out of the water (missing our marcke) whereat we directed our leuell, which otherwise we should hardly recouer, and oftentimes the restore to vs our shaftes which we thought neuer to see, touche or handle againe, after they were lost, for which circum-staunces they are called *Inquisitores*, searchers, and finders. Although the ducke otherwhiles notably deceaueth both the dogge and the master, by dyuing vnder the water, and also by naturall subtilty, for if any man shall approche to the place where they builde, breede, and syt, the hennes go out of their neastes, offering themselues voluntarily to the hāds, as it were, of such as draw nie their neastes. And a certaine weaknesse of their winges pretended, and infirmitie of their feete dissembled, they go so slowely and so leasurely, that to a mans thinking it were no masteryes

to take them. By which deceiptfull tricke they doe as it were entyse
and allure men to follow them, till they be drawne a long distaunce
from theyr neastes, which being compassed by their prouident conning, or conning providence they cut of all inconueniences which might
growe of their returne, by using many carefull and curious caucates, least
theyr often haunting bewray yᵉ place where the young ducklings be
hatched. Great therefore is theyr desire, & earnest is theyr study to
take heede, not only to theyr broode but also to themselues. For when
they haue an ynkling that they are espied they hide themselves vnder
turfes or sedges, wherewith they couer and shrowde themselues so closely
and so craftely, that (notwithstanding the place where they lurke be
found and perfectly perceaued) there they will harbour without harme,
except the water spaniell by quicke smelling discouer theyr deceiptes.

Of the Dogge called the Fisher, in Latine
Canis Piscator.

THe Dogge called the fisher, whereof Hector Boethus writeth, which
seeketh for fishe by smelling among rockes & stones, assuredly I
knowe none of that kinde in Englande, neither haue I receaued by reporte
that there is any suche, albeit I haue been diligent & busie in demaunding
the question as well of fishermen, as also of huntesmen in that behalfe
being carefull and earnest to learne and vnderstand of them if any such
were, except you holde opinion that the beauer or Otter is a fishe (as many
haue beleened) & according to their beliefe affirmed, and as the birde
Pupine, is thought to be a fishe and so accounted. But that kinde of
dogge which followeth the fishe to apprehend and take it (if there bee any
of that disposition and property) whether they do this for the game of
hunting, or for the heate of hunger, as other Dogges do which rather then
they wil be famished for want of foode, couet the carckases of carrion and

putrifyed fleshe. When I am fully resolued and disburthened of this
doubt I wil send you certificate in writing. In the meane season I am
not ignorant of that both *Ælianus,* and *Ælius* call the Beauer κὺνατοτάμιον
a water dogge, or a dogge fishe, I know likewise thus much more, that
the Beauer doth participate this propertie with the dogge, namely, that
when fishes be scarse they leaue the water and raunge vp and downe the
lande, making an insatiable slaughter of young lembes vntil theyr
paunches be replenished, and whē they haue fed themselues full of fleshe,
then returne they to the water, from whence they came. But albeit so
much be graunted that this Beauer is a dogge, yet it is to be noted that we
recken it not in the beadrowe of Englishe dogges as we haue done the
rest. The sea Calfe, in like maner, which our country mō for breuitie
sake call a Seele, other more largely name a *Sea Vele* maketh a spoyle of
fishes betweene rockes and banckes, but it is not accounted in the
catalogue or nūber of our Englishe dogges, notwithstanding we call it by
the name of a Sea dogge or a sea Calfe. And thus much for our dogges
of the second sort called in Latine *Acvpatorij,* seruing to take fowle
either by land or water.

¶ A Diall pertaining to the
fecond Section

Dogges seruing the disport of fowling.	are diuided into	Land spaniels Setters Water spaniels or finders.	called in latine *Canes Au cupatorij*	The fisher is not of their number but seuerall.

The thirde Section of this
abridgement.

*Owe followeth in due order and con-*venient place our Englishe Dogges of the thirde gentle kinde, what they are called to what vse they serue, and what sort of people plant their pleasure in thẽ, which because they neede no curious cannassing and nye syfting, wee meane to bee so much the briefer.

Of the delicate, neate, and pretty kind of dogges
called the Spaniel gentle, or the comforter, in Latine *Melitæus*
or Fotor.

THere is, besides those which wee haue already deliuered, another sort of gentle dogges in this our Englishe soyle but exempted from the order of the residue, the Dogges of this kinde doth *Callimachus* call *Melitæos*, of the Iseland Melita, in the sea of *Sicily*, (what at this day is named *Malta*, an Iseland in deede famous and renoumed, with couragious and puisaunt souldiours valliauntly fighting vnder the banner of Christ their vnconquerable captaine) where this kind of dogges had their principall beginning.

These dogges are litle, pretty, proper, and fyne, and sought for to satisfie the delicatenesse of daintie dames, and wanton womens wills, in-strumentes of folly for them to play and dally withall, to tryfle away the treasure of time, to withdraw their mindes from more commendable

exercises, and to content their corrupted concupiscences with vaine disport (A selly shift to shunne yrcksome ydlnesse.) These puppies the
smaller they be, the more pleasure they prouoke, as more meete play
fellowes for minsing mistrisses to beare in their bosoms, to keepe company withal in their chambers, to succour with sleepe in bed, and nourishe
with meate at bourde, to lay in their lappes, and licke their lippes as
they ryde in their waggons, and good reason it should be so, for course-
nesse with fynenesse hath no fellowship, but featnesse with neatenesse
hath neighbourhood enough. That plausible prouerbe verified vpon a
Tyraunt, namely that he loued his sowe better then his sonne, may well
be applyed to these kinde of people, who delight more in dogges that are
depriued of all possibility of reason, then they doe in children that be
capeable of wisedome and iudgement. But this abuse peraduenture
raigneth where there hath bene long lacke of issue, or else where barren-
nes is the best blossome of bewty.

The vertue which remaineth in the Spaniell gentle
otherwise called the comforter.

NOtwithstanding many make much of those pretty puppies called
Spaniells gentle, yet if the question were demaunded what propertie
in them they spye, which shoulde make them so acceptable and precious
in their sight, I doubt their aunswere would be long a coyning. But
seeing it was our intent to trauaile in this treatise, so that y⁰ reader
might reape some benefite by his reading, we will communicate vnto you
such coniecures as are grounded vpon reason. And though some suppose
that such dogges are fyt for no seruice, I dare say, by their leaues, they
be in a wrong boxe. Among all other qualities therefore of nature, which
be knowne (for some conditions are couered with continuall and thicke
clouds, that the eye of our capacities cannot pearse through thē) we find

that these litle doges are good to asswage the sicknesse of the stomacke
being oftentimes therevnto applyed as a plaster preseruatiue, or borne
in the bosom of the diseased and weake person, which effect is performed by theyr moderate heate. Moreouer the disease and sicknesse,
channgeth his place and entreth (though it be not precisely marcked)
into the dogge, which to be no vntruth, experience can testify, for these
kinde of dogges sometimes fall sicke, and sometime die, without any
harm, outwardly inforced, which is an argument that the disease of the
gentleman or gentle woman or owner whatsoeuer, entreth into the dogge
by the operation of heate intermingled and infected. And thus haue I
hetherto handled dogges of a gentle kinde whom I haue comprehended
in a triple diuisiō. Now it remaineth that I annex in due order such
dogges as be of a more homely kinde.

A Diall pertaining to the
thirde Section.

In the third section is cō-tained one kind of dog which is cal led the	Spaniell gentle or the cō-forter,	It is also called	A chamber cō-panion A pleasannt playfellow, A pretty worme	gene-rally called *Canis delica-tus.*

i

The fourth Section of this
difcourfe

Dogges of a Course Kind seruing for many Necessary uses,
called in Latine *Canes Ruftici*, and first of the
shepherds dogge, called in Latine
Canis Paftoralis.

Dogges of   { The shepherds dogge } These two are
the courser { The maftine or   } the principall.
sort are   { Bandogge.   }

He firft kinde, namely the fhepherds hounde is very necessarye and profitable for the auoyding of harmes and inconueniences which may come to men by the means of beastes. The second sort serue to succour against the snares and attemptes of mischiefous men. Our shepherdes dogge is not huge, vaste, and bigge, but of an indifferent stature and growth, because it hath not to deale with the bloudthyrsty wolf, sythence there be none in England, which happy and fortunate benefite is to be ascribed to the puisaunt Prince *Edgar*, who to thintent ye the whole countrey myght be euacuated and quite clered from wolfes, charged & commaunded the welshemā (who were pestered with these butcherly beastes aboue measure) to paye him yearely tribute which was (note the wisedome of the King) three hundred Wolfes. Some there be which write that *Ludwall* Prince of Wales paide yeerly to King *Edgar* three hundred wolves in the name of an exaction (as we haue sayd before.) And that by the meanes

D

hereof, within the compasse and tearme of foure yeares none of those noysome, and pestilent Beastes were left in the coastes of England and Wales. This *Edgar* wore the Crown royall, and bare the Scepter imperiall of this kingdome, about the yeere of our Lorde nyne hundred fifty, nyne. Synce which time we reede that no Wolfe hath bene seene in England, bred within the bounds and borders of this countrey, mary there have bene diuers brought ouer from beyonde the seas, for greedynesse of gaine and to make money, for gasing and gaping, staring, and standing to see them, being a straunge beast, rare, and seldom seene in England. But to returne to our shepherds dogge. This dogge either at the hearing of his masters voyce, or at the wagging and whisteling in his fist, or at his shrill and horse hissing bringeth the wandring weathers and straying sheepe, into the selfe same place where his masters will and wishe, is to haue the, wherby the shepherd reapeth this benefite, namely, that with litle labour and no toyle or mouing of his feete he may rule and guide his flocke, according to his owne desire, either to haue them go forward, or to stand still, or to drawe backward, or to turne this way, or to take that way. For it is not in Englande, as it is in *Fraunce*, as it is in *Flaunders*, as it is in *Syria*, as it in *Tartaria*, where the sheepe follow the shepherd, for heere in our country the sheepherd followeth the sheepe. And sometimes the straying sheepe, when no dogge runneth before them, nor goeth about & beside them, gather themselues together in a flocke, when they heere the sheepherd whistle in his fist, for feare of the Dogge (as I imagine) remembring this (if vnreasonable creatures may be reported to haue memory) that the Dogge commonly runneth out at his masters warrant which is his whistle. This haue we oftentimes diligently marcked in taking our journey from towne to towne, when wee haue hard a sheepherd whistle we haue rayned in our horse and stoode styll a space, to see the proofe and triall of this matter. Furthermore with this dogge doth the sheepherd take sheepe for yᵉ slaughter, and to be healed if they be sicke, no hurt or harme in the world done to the simple creature.

Of the mastiue or Bandogge called in Latine
Villaticus or *Cathenarius.*

THis kinde of Dogge called a mastyne or Bandogge is vaste, huge, stubborne, ougly, and eager, of a heuy and burthenous body, and therefore but of litle swiftnesse, terrible, and frightfull to beholde, and more fearce and fell then any *Arcadian* curre (notwithstäding they are sayd to haue their generation of the violent Lion.) They are called *Villatici*, because they are appoynted to watche and keepe farme places and coûtry cotages sequestred from commõ recourse, and not abutting vpon other houses by reason of distaunce, when there is any feare conceaued of theefes, robbers, spoylers, and night wanderers. They are seruiceable against the Foxe and the Badger, to drive wilde and tame swyne out of Medowes, pastures, glebelandes and places planted with fruite, to bayte and take the bull by the eare, when occasion so requireth. One dogge or two at the vttermost, sufficient for that purpose be the bull neuer so monsterous, neuer so fearce, neuer so furious, neuer so stearne, neuer so vntameable. For it is a kinde of dogge capeable of courage, violent and valiaunt, striking could feare into the harts of men, but standing in feare of no man, in so much that no weapons will make him shrincke, nor abridge his boldnes. Our Englishe men (to th' intent that theyr dogges might be the more fell and fearce) assist nature with arte, vse, and custome, for they teach theyr dogges to baite the Beare, to baite the Bull and other such like cruell and bloudy beastes (appointing an ouerseer of the game) without any collar to defend theyr throtes, and oftentimes they traine them vp in fighting and wrestling with a man hauing for the safegarde of his lyfe, eyther a Pikestaffe, a clubbe, or a sworde and by vsing them to such exercises as these, theyr dogges become more sturdy and strong. The force which is in them surmounteth all beleefe, the fast holde which they take with their teeth exceedeth all credit, three of them against a Beare, fowre against a Lyon are sufficient, both to try masteryes with them and vtterly to oucrmatch them. Which *Henry* the seuenth of that name, King of England (a Prince both politique & warlike) perceauing on a certaine time (as the report runneth) commaunded all such dogges (how many soeuer they were in number) should be hanged, beyng deepely displeased, and conceauing great disdaine that an yll faured rascall curre should with such violent villany, assault the valiaunt Lyon king of all beastes. An example for all subiects worthy remembraunce, to admonishe them that it is no aduantage to them to rebell against ye regiment of their ruler, but to keepe them within the limits of Loyaltie. I reede an history aunswerable to this of the selfe same *Henry*, who hauing a notable and an excellent fayre Falcon, it fortuned that the kings Falconers, in the presence and hearing of his grace, highly commended his Maiesties Falcon, saying that it feared not to intermeddle with an Eagle, it was so venturous a byrde and so mighty, which when the King harde, he charged that the Falcon should be killed without delay, for the selfe same reason (as it may seeme) which was rehersed in the coclusion of the former history concerning the same king. This dogge is called, in like maner, *Cathenarius, a Cathena*, of the chaine wherwith he is tyed at the gates, in ye daytime, least beyng lose he should doe much mischiefe and yet might giue occasion of feare and terror by his bigge barcking. And albeit *Cicero* in his oration had *Pro. S. Ross.* be of this opinion, that such Dogges as barcke in the broade day light shoulde haue their legges broken, yet our countrymen, on this side the seas for their carelessnes of lyfe setting all at cinque and sice, are of a contrary iudgement. For theefes roge vp and down in euery corner, no place is free from them, no not ye prince's pallace, nor the country mans cotage. In the day time they practise pilfering, picking, open robbing, and priuy stealing, and what legerdemaine lacke they : not fearing the shamefull and horrible death of hanging. The cause of which inconuenience doth not onely issue from nipping neede & wringing want, for all yᵉ steale, are not pinched with pouerty, but som steale to maintaine their excessive and prodigall expences in apparell, their lewdnes of lyfe, their hautines of hart, theyr wantonnes of maners, theyr wilfull ydlenes, their ambitious brauery, and the pryde of the sawcy *Salacones'* μιγαλοῤῥοῦτον vaine glorious and arrogant in behauiour, whose delight dependeth wholly to mount nimbly on horsebacke, to make them leape lustely, spryng and praunce, galloppe and amble, to runne a race, to wynde in compasse, and so forthe, lining all together vpon the fatnesse of the spoyle. Other som ther be which steale, being thereto prouoked by penury & neede, like masterlesse mē applying themselues to no honest trade, but raunging vp and downe impudently begging, and complayning of bodily weakenesse where is no want of abilitie. But valiaunt *Valentine* th'emperour, by holsome lawes prouided that suche as hauing no corporall sicknesse, solde themselues to begging, pleded pouerty wyth pretended infirmitie, & cloaked their ydle and slouthfull life with colourable shifts and cloudy cossening, should be a perpetuall slaue and drudge to him, by whom their impudent ydlenes was bewrayed, and layed against them in publique place, least the insufferable slouthfullnes of such vagabondes should be burthenous to the people, or being so hatefull and odious, should growe into an example. *Alfredus* likewise in the gouernment of his commonwealth, procured such increase of credite to iustice and upright dealing by his prudent actes and statutes, that if a mā trauailing by the hygh way of the countrey vnder his dominion, chaunced to lose a budget full of gold, or his capcase farsed with things of great value, late in the euening, he shoulde find it where he lost it, safe, sound, and vntouched the next morning, yea (which is a wonder) at any time for a whole monethes space if he sought for it, as *Ingulphus*

Croyladensis in his Hystory recordeth. But in this our vnhappy age, in these (I say) our denelishe dayes nothing can scape the clawes of the spoyler, though it be kept neuer so sure within the house, albeit the doores bee lockt and boulted round about. This dogge in like maner of *Grecians* is called *οἰκουρός*

Of the latinists *Canis Cultos*, in Englishe
the Dogge keeper.

Borrowing his name of his seruice, for he doth not onely keepe farmers houses, but also merchaunts maisons, wherin great wealth, riches, sub-staunce and costly stuffe is reposed. And therfore were certain dogges founde and maintained at the common costes and charges of the Citizens of *Rome* in the place called *Capitolium*, to giue warning of theefes comming. This kind of dogge, is also called,

In latine *Canis Lantarius* in Englishe the
Butchers Dogge

So called for the necessity of his vse, for his seruice affoordeth great benefite to the Butcher as well in following as in taking his cattell when neede constraineth, vrgeth, and requireth. This kinde of dogge is like-wise called,

In latine *Molosscicus* or *Molossus*.

After the name of a countrey in *Epirus* called *Molossia*, which harboureth many stoute, stronge, and sturdy Dogges of this sort, for the dogges of that countrey are good in deede, or else there is no trust to be had in the testimonie of writers. This dogge is also called,

In latine *Canis Mandatarius* a Dogge messinger or Carrier.

Upon substanciall consideration, because at his masters voyce and commaundement, he carrieth letters from place to place, wrapped vp cunningly in his lether collar, fastened thereto, or sowed close therin, who, least he should be hindered in his passage vseth these helpes very skilfully, namely resistaunce in fighting if he be not ouermatched, or else swiftnesse & readinesse in running away, if he be vnable to buckle with the dogge that would faine have a snatch at his skinne   This kinde of dogge is also called,

In latine *Canis Lunarius,* in Englishe
the Mooner.

Because he doth nothing else but watch and warde at an ynche, wasting the wearisome night season without slombering or sleeping, bawing & wawing at the Moone (that I may vse the word of *Nonius*) a qualitie in mine opinion straunge to consider.   This kinde of dogge is also called,

In latine *Aquarius* in Englishe a water drawer.

And these be of the greater and the waighter sort drawing water out of wells and deepe pittes, by a wheele which they turne rounde about by the mouing of their burthenous bodies.   This kinde of dogge is called in like maner.

Canis Sarcinarius in Latine, and may aptly be eng-
lished a Tynckers Curre.

Because with marueilous pacience they beare bigge budgettes fraught with Tinckers tooles, and mettall meete to mend kettles, porrige pottes, skellets, and chafers, and other such like trumpery requisite for their occupacion and loytering trade, easing him of a great burthen which otherwise he himselfe should carry vpon his shoulders, which condition hath challenged vnto them the foresaid name.   Besides the qualities which we haue already recounted, this kind of dogges hath this prin-cipall propertie ingrafted in them, that they loue their masters liberally, and hate straungers despightfully, wherevpon it followeth that they are to their masters, in traueiling a singular safgard, defending them force-ably, from the inuasion of villons and theefes, preseruing their lyfes from losse, and their health from hassard, theyr fleshe from hacking and hewing with such like desperate daungers,　For which consideration they are meritoriously tearmed,

In Latine *Canes defenſores* defending dogges
in our mother toungue.

If it chaunce that the master bee oppressed, either by a multitude, or by the greater violence & so be beaten downe that he lye groueling on the grounde, (it is proued true by experience) that this Dogge forsaketh not his master, no not when he is starcke deade : But induring the force of famishment and the outrageous tempestes of the weather, most vigilantly watcheth and carefully keepeth the deade carkasse many dayes, endeuouring, furthermore, to kil the murtherer of his master, if he may get any advantage.　Or else by barcking, by howling, by furious iarring, snarring, and such like meanes betrayeth the malefactour as desirous to haue the death of his aforesayde Master rigorouslye reuenged.　And example hereof fortuned within the compasse of my memory.　The Dogge of a certaine wayefaring man tranailing from the Citie of London directly to the Towne of Kingstone (most famous and renowned by reason of the triumphant coronation of eight seuerall Kings) passing ouer a good portion of his iourney was assaulted and set vpon by certaine confederate theefes laying in waight for the spoyle in *Comeparcke,* a perillous bottom, compassed about wyth woddes to well knowne for the manyfolde murders & mischiefeous robberies theyr committed.　Into whose handes this passinger chaunced to fall, so that his ill lucke cost him the price of his lyfe.　And that Dogge whose syer was Englishe (which *Blondus* registreth to haue bene within the banckes of his remēbrance) manifestly perceauyng that his Master was murthered (this chaunced not farre from *Paris,* by the handes of one which was a suiter to the same womā, whom he was a wooer unto, dyd both bewraye the bloudy butcher, and attempted to teare out the villons throate if he had not sought meanes to auoyde the reuenging rage of the Dogge.　In fyers also which fortune in the silence and dead time of the night, or in stormy weather of the sayde season, the older dogges barcke, ball, howle, and yell (yea notwithstandyng they bee roughly rated) neyther will they stay their tounges till the householde seruauntes awake, ryse, search, and see the burning of the fyre, which beyng perceaued they vse voluntary silence, and cease from yolping This hath bene, and is founde true by tryall, in sundry partes of England. There was no faynting faith in that Dogge, which when his Master by a mischaunce in hunting stumbled and fell toppling downe a deepe dytche beyng vnable to recouer of himselfe, the Dogge signifying his masters mishappe, reskue came, and he was hayled up by a rope, whom the Dogge seeying almost drawne up to the edge of the dytche, cheerefully saluted, leaping and skipping vpon his master as though he woulde haue imbraced hym, beyng glad of his presence, whose longer absence he was lothe to lacke. Some Dogges there be, which will not suffer fyery coales to lye skattered about the hearthe, but with their pawes wil rake up the burnyng coales, musying and studying fyrst with themselues how it might be conueniently be done. And if so bee that the coales caste to great a heate then will they buyry them in ashes and so remoue them forwarde to a fyt place wyth theyr noses. Other Dogges bee there which exequute the office of a Farmer in the nyghte tyme. For when his master goeth to bedde to take his naturall sleepe, And when,

> A hundred barres of brasse and yron boltes,
> Make all things safe from startes and from reuoltes.
> VVhen Ianus keepes the gate with Argos eye,
> That daungers none approch, ne mischiefes nye.

As Virgill vaunteth in his verses, Then if his master byddeth him go abroade, he lingereth not, but raungeth ouer all his lands lying there about, more diligently, I wys, then any farmer himselfe. And if he finde anything their that is straunge and pertaining to other persons besides

his master, whether it be man, woman, or beast, he driueth them out of
the ground, not meddling with any thing which doth belong to the
possession and vse of his master, But how much faythfulnes, so much
diuersitie there is in their natures,

For there
be some,

{
Which barcke only with free and open
  throate but will not bite,
Which doe both barcke and byte,
Which bite bitterly before they barcke,
}

The first are not greatly to be feared, because they themselues are
fearefull, and fearefull dogges (as the prouerbe importeth) barcke most
vehemently.

The second are daungerous, it is wisedome to take heede of them because they sounde, as it were, an *Alarum* of an afterclappe, and these
dogges must not be ouer much moued or pronoked, for then they take
on outragiously as if they were madde, watching to set the print of their
teeth in the fleshe.   And these kinde of dogges are fearce and eager by
nature.

The thirde are deadly, for they flye upon a man, without vtteraunce of
voyce, snatch at him, and catche him by the throate, and most cruelly
byte out colloppes of fleashe. Feare these kind of Curres (if thou bee wise
and circumspect about thine owne safetie) for they be stoute and stubborne
dogges, and set vpon a man at a sodden vnwares.   By these signes and
tokens, by these notes and arguementes our men discerne the cowardly
curre from the couragious dogge the bolde from the fearefull, the
butcherly from the gentle and tractable,   Moreouer they coniecture that
a whelpe of an yll kinde is not worthe the keeping and that no dogge
can serue the sundry vses of men so aptly and so conueniently as this
sort of whom we haue so largely written already.   For if any be disposed
to drawe the aboue named seruices into a table, what mã more clearely,
and with more vehemency of voyce giueth warning eyther of a wastefull
beaste, or of a spoiling theefe than this ? who by his barcking (as good as

a burning beacon) foreshoweth hassards at hand? What maner of beast stronger? what seruaũt to his master more louing? what companion more trustie? what watchman more vigilant? what reuenger more constant? what messinger more speedie? what water bearer more painefull? Finally what packhorse more patient? And thus much concerning English Dogges, first of the gentle kinde, secondly of the courser kinde. Nowe it remaineth that we deliuer vnto you the Dogges of a mungrell or a currishe kinde, and then will wee perfourme our taske.

¶ A Diall pertaining to the
fourth Section.

Dogs comprehended in yᵉ fourth secion are these
{
The shepherds dogge
The Mastiue or Bandogge
}
which hath sundry names deriued frõ sun dry circustances as
{
The keeper or watchman
The butchers dogge
The messinger or carrier
The Mooner
The water drawer
The Tinckers curr
The fencer,
}

{
called in Latine *Canes Rustici.*
}

The fifth Section of this
treatiſe.

Containing Curres of the mungrell and rascall sort and
first of the Dogge called in Latine, *Admonitor*
and of vs in Englishe VVappe
or VVarner.

F such dogges as keep not their kinde,
of such as are mingled out of sundry sortes not
imitating the conditions of some one certaine
spice, because they reſeble no notable shape, nor
exercise any worthy property of the true perfect
and gentle kind, it is not necessarye that I write
any more of them, but to banishe them as vnpro-
fitable implements, out of the boundes of my Booke, vnprofitable I say
for any use that is commendable, except to intertaine straũgers with their
barcking in the day time, giuing warnyng to them of the house, that such
& such be newly come, wherevpon wee call them admonishing Dogges,
because in that point they performe theyr office.

Of the Dogge called Turnespete in Latine *Vcruuersator.*

THere is comprehended, vnder the curres of the coursest kinde, a
certaine dogge in kytchen seruice excellent. For whũ any meate is
to bee roasted they go into a wheele which they turning rounde about
with the waight of their bodies, so diligently looke to their businesse,

that no drudge nor skullion can doe the feate more cunningly. Whom the popular sort herevpon call Turnespets, being the last of all those which wee haue first mencioned.

Of the Dogge called the Daunser, in Latine
Saltator or *Tympanista.*

THere be also dogges among vs of a mungrell kind which are taught and exercised to daunce in measure at the musicall sounde of an instrument, as, at the iust stroke of the drombe, at the sweete accent of the Cyterne, & tuned strings of the harmonious Harpe showing many pretty trickes by the gesture of their bodies. As to stand bolte upright, to lye flat vpon the grounde, to turne rounde as a ringe holding their tailes in their teeth, to begge for theyr meate, and sundry such properties, which they learne of theyr vagabundicall masters, whose instrumentes they are to gather gaine, withall in Citie, Country, Towne, and Village. As some which carry olde apes on their shoulders in coloured iackets to moue men to laughter for a litle lucre.

Of other Dogges, a short conclusion, wonderfully in-gendred within the coastes of this country.

Three sortes of them,	The first bred of a bytch and a wolfe,	In Latine *Lyciscus.*
	The second of a bytyche and a foxe,	In Latine *Lacœna.*
	The third of a beare and a bandogge,	In Latine *Vrcanus.*

OF the first we haue none naturally bred within the borders of Eng-land. The reason is for the want of wolfes, without whom no such kinde of dog can bee ingendred. Againe it is deliuered unto thee in this discourse, how and by what meanes, by whose benefitte, and within what circuite of tyme, this country was cleerely discharged of rauenyng wolfes, and none at all left, no, not to the least number, or the beginnyng of a number, which is an *Vnari*.

Of the second sort we are not vtterly voyde of some, because this our Englishe soyle is not free from foxes (for in deede we are not without a multitude of them in so much as diuerse keepe, foster, and feede them in their houses among their houndes and dogges, eyther for some maladie of mind, or for some sicknesse of body,) which peraduenture the savour of that subtill beast would eyther mitigate or expell.

The thirde kinde which is bred of a Beare and a Bandogge we want not heare in England, (A straunge and wonderfull effect, that cruell enimyes should enter into ye worke of copulation & bring forth so sauage a curre.) Undoubtedly it is euen so as we haue reported, for the fyery heate of theyr fleshe, or rather the pricking thorne, or most of all, the tyckling lust of lechery, beareth such swinge and sway in them, that there is no contrairietie for the time, but of constraint they must ioyne to ingender. And why should not this bee consonant to truth ? why shoulde not these beastes breede in this lande, as well as in other forreigne nations ? For wee reede that Tigers and dogges in *Hircania*, that Lyons and Dogges in *Arcadia*, and that wolfes and dogges in *Francia*, couple and procreate. In men and women also lyghtened with the lantarne of reason (but vtterly voide of vertue) that foolishe, frantique, and fleshely action, yet naturally sealed in vs) worketh so effectuously, & many tymes it doth reconcile enimyes, set foes at freend-ship, vnanimitie, and atonement, as *Moria* mencioneth. The *Vrcane* which is bred of a beare and a dogge,

> Is fearce, is fell, is stoute and stronge,
> And byteth sore to fleshe and bone,
> His furious force indureth longe
> In rage he will be rul'de of none.

That I may vse the wordes of the Poet *Gratius.* This dogge exceedeth all other in cruell conditions, his leering and fleering lookes, his stearne and sauage vissage, maketh him in sight fearefull and terrible, he is violent in fighting, & wheresoeuer he setteth his tenterhooke teeth, he taketh such sure & fast holde, that a man may sooner teare and rende him in sunder, then lose him and seperate his chappes. He passeth not for the Wolfe, the Beare, the Lyon, nor the Bulle and may wortherly (as I think,) be companpiō with *Alexanders* dogge which came out of *India.* But of these, thus much, and thus farre may seeme sufficient.

A starte to outlandishe Dogges in this conclusion,
not impertinent to the Authors purpose.

VSe and custome hath intertained other dogges of an outlandishe kinde, but a fewe and the same beyng of a pretty bygnesse, I meane Iseland, dogges curled & rough al ouer, which by reason of the lenght of their heare make showe neither of face nor of body. And yet these curres, forsoothe, because they are so straunge are greatly set by, esteemed, taken vp, and made of many times in the roome of the Spaniell gentle or comforter. The natures of men is so moued, nay rather marryed to nouelties without all reason, wyt, iudgement or perseueraunce. Ερωμεν αλλοτριαν, παροραμεν συγγενις.

Outlandishe toyes we take with delight
Things of our owne nation we haue in despight.

Which fault remaineth not in vs concerning dogges only, but for artificers also. And why? it is to manyfest that wee disdayne and contempne our owne workmen, be they neuer so skilfull, be they neuer so cunning, be they neuer so excellent. A beggerly beast brought out of barbarous borders, fro' the vttermost countryes Northward, &c., we stare at, we gase at, we muse, we maruaile at, like an asse of *Cumanum,* like Thales with the brasen shancks, like the man in the Moone.

The which default *Hippocrates* marcked when he was alyne as euidently appeareth in the beginnyng of his booke περὶ ἀγμῶν so intituled and named :

And we in our worcke entituled *De Ephemera Britanica*, to the people of England haue more plentifully expressed. In this kinde looke which is most blocklishe, and yet most waspishe, the same is most estcemed, and not amonge Citizens onely and iolly gentlemen, but amonge lustie Lordes also, and noble men, and daintie courtier ruffling in their ryotous ragges. Further I am not to wade in the foorde of this discourse, because it was my purpose to satisfie your expectation with a short treatise (most learned *Conrade*) not wearysome for me to wryte, nor tedious for you to peruse. Among other things which you haue receaued at my handes heretofore, I remember that I wrote a seuerall description of the *Getulian* Dogge, because there are but a fewe of them and therefore very seldome seene. As touching Dogges of other kyndes you your selfe haue taken earnest paine, in writing of them both lyuely, learnedly and largely. But because wee haue drawne this libell more at length then the former which I sent you (and yet briefer than the nature of the thing myght well beare) regardyng your more earnest and necessary studdies. I will conclude makyng a rehearsall notwithstanding (for memoryes sake) of certaine specialties contayned in the whole bcdy of this my breuiary. And because you participate principall pleasure, in the knowledge in the common and vsuall names of Dogges (as I gather by the course of your letters) I suppose it not amysse to deliuer vnto you a shorte table contayning as well the Latine as the Englishe names, and to render a reason of euery particular appellation, to th'intent that no scruple may remaine in this point, but that euery thing may bee sifted to the bare bottome.

A Diall pertaining to the
Fifte Section.

Dogges contained in this last Diall or Table are	The Wapp or Warner, The Turnespet, The dauncer,	called in Latine *Canes Rustici*

A Supplement or Addition contai-
ning a demonftration of Dogges
names how they had their
Originall.

He names contayned in the generall
table, for so much as they signifie nothing to
you being a straunger, and ignoraunt of the
Englishe tounge, except they be interpreted :
As we haue giuen a reason before of ye latine
words so mean we to doe no lesse of the Englishe, that euery thing maye be manyfest unto
your vnderstanding.   Wherein I intende to obserue the same order
which I haue followed before.

The names of such Dogges as be contained in
the first section.

Agax, in Englishe Hunde, is deriued of our English word hunte.
One letter chaunged in another, namely T, into D, as Hunt, Hunde,

whom (if you coniecture to be so named of your country worde *Hunde* which signifieth the generall name Dogge, because of the similitude and likenesse of the wordes I will not stand in contradiction (friend *Gesner*) for so muche as we retaine among vs to this day many Dutche wordes which the *Saxons* left at such time as they occupyed this country of Britane. Thus much also vnderstand, that as in your language *Hunde* is the common word, so in our naturall tounge dogge is the vniuersall, but *Hunde* is perticular and a speciall, for it signifieth such a dogge onely as serueth to hunt, and therefore it is called a hunde.

Of the Gasehound.

The Gasehounde called in latine *Agasæus*, hath his name of the sharpnesse and stedfastnesse of his eyesight. By which vertue he compasseth that which otherwise he cannot by smelling attaine. As we haue made former relation for to gase is earnestly to viewe and beholde, from whence floweth the deriuation of this dogges name.

Of the Grehounde.

The Grehounde called *Leporarius*, hath his name of this word, Gre, which word soundeth *Gradus* in latine, in Englishe degree. Because among all dogges these are the most principall, occupying the chiefest place, and being simply and absolutely the best of the gentle kinde of houndes.

Of the Leuyuer or the Lyemmer.

This dogge is called a Lenyner, for his lightnesse, which in latine soundeth *Leuitas*, Or a Lyemmer which worde is borrowed of Lyemme which the latinists name *Lorum*; and wherefore we call him a Leuyner of this worde *Leuitas* (as we doe many things besides) why we deriue and drawe a thousand of our tearmes out of the *Greeke*, the *Latine*, the *Italian*, the *Dutch*, the *French*, and the *Spanishe* tounge : (Out of which fountaines indeede, they had their originall issue.) How many words are buryed in the grave of forgetfullnes? growne out of vse? wrested

awrye and peruersly corrupted by diuers defaultes ? we wil declare at
large in our booke intituled, *Simphonia vocum Britannicarum.*

Of the Tumbler.

Among houndes the Tumbler called in latine *Vertagus,* is the last, which
commeth of this worde Tumbler flowing first of al out of the French
fountaine. For as we say Tumble so they *Tumbier,* reseruing one sense
and signification, which the latinists comprehende vnder this worde
Vertere, So that we see thus much, that Tumbler commeth of *Tumbier,*
the vowel, I, chaunged into the *Liquid* L, after ye maner of our speache,
Contrary to the French and the Italian tounge. In which two languages,
A *Liquid* before a *Vowell* for the most part is turned into another
Vowell, As, may be perceaued in the example of these two wordes,
Implere & plano, for *Impiere & piano,* L, before, E chaunged into, I,
and L, before A, turned into I, also. This I thought conuenient for
a taste.

The names of such Dogges as be contained in
the second Section.

AFter such as serue for hunting orderly doe follow such as serue for
hawking and fowling. Among which the principall and chiefest is
the Spaniell, called in Latine *Hispaniolus,* borrowing his name of
Hispania Spaine, wherein wee Englishe men not pronouncing the Aspira-
tion H, Nor the *Vowell* I, for quicknesse and redinesse of speach say
roundly A Spaniell.

Of the Setter.

The second sorte of this second division and second section, is called a
Setter, in latine *Index,* Of the worde Set which signifieth in Englishe that
which the Latinistes meane by this word *Locum designare,* ye reason is
rehersed before more largely, it shall not neede to make a new repeti-
tion.

Of the water Spaniell or Finder.

The water Spaniell consequently followeth, called in Latine *Aquaticus*, in English a water spaniell, which name is compounde of two simple wordes, namely Water, which in Latine soûdeth *Aqua*, wherein he swymmeth. And *Spaine Hispania*, the country frõ whence they came, Not that England wanted such kinde of Dogges, (for they are naturally bred and ingendred in this country.) But because they beare the generall and common name of these Dogges synce the time they were first brought ouer out of Spaine. And wee make a certaine difference in this sort of Dogges, eyther for some thing which in theyr voyce is to be marked, or for something which in their qualities is to be considered, as for an example in this kinde called the Spaniell by the apposition and putting to of this word water, which two coupled together sounde water-spaniell. He is also called a fynder, in Latine *Inquisitor*, because that by serious and secure seeking, he findeth such things as be lost, which word *Finde* in Englishe is that which the Latines meane by this Verbe *Inuenire* This dogge hath this name of his property because the principall point of his seruice consisteth in the premisses.

The names of such Dogges as be contained in
the thirde Section.

NOw leauing tho seruic we of hunting and hauking dogs, it remaineth that we runne ouer the residue, whereof some be called, fine dogs, some course, other some mungrels or rascalls. The first is the Spaniell gentle called *Canis Meliteus*, because it is a kinde of dogge accepted among gentles, Nobles, Lordes, Ladies, &c., who make much of them vouchsafeing to admit them so farre into their company, that they will not onely lull them in theyr lappes, but kysse them with their lippes, and make them theyr prettie playfellowes. Such a one was

Gorgons litle puppie mencioned by *Theocritus Siracusis,* who taking his
iourney, straightly charged & commaunded his mayde to see to his
Dogge as charely and warely as to his childe : To call him in alwayes
that he wandred not abroade, as well as to rock the babe a sleepe, crying
in the cradle. This puppitly and peasantly curre, (which some frump-
ingly tearme fysteing hounds) serue in a maner to no good vse except,
(As we haue made former relation) to succour and strengthen quailing
and quammning stomackes to bewray bawdery, and filthy abbominable
lewdnesse (whiche a litle dogge of this kinde did in *Sicilia*) as *Ælianus*
in his, 7, book of beastes, and 27, chapter recordeth.

The names of such dogges as be contained in
the fourth Section.

O F dogges vnder the courser kinde, we will deale first with the
shepherds dogge, whom we call the Bandogge, the Tydogge, or
the Mastyue, the first name is imputed to him for service *Quoniam
pastori famulatur,* because he is at the shepherds his masters commaundement. The seconde a *Ligamento* of the band or chaine wherewith
he is tyed. The thirde a *Sagina,* of the fatnesse of his body.

For this kinde of dogge which is vsually tyed, is myghty, grosse, and
fat fed. I know this that *Augustinus Niphus* calleth this *Mastinus*
(which we call Mastiuus.) And that *Albertus* wrīteth how the *Lyciscus* is
ingendred by a beare and a wolfe. Notwithstanding the self same Author
taketh it for the most part *pro Molosso.* A dogge of such a countrey.

The names of such dogges as be contained in
the fifte Section.

O F mungrels and rascalls somwhat is to be spoken. And among
these, of ye *VVappe* or *Turnespet* which name is made of two

simple words, that is of *Turne* which in Latine soundeth *Vertere*, and of *spete* which is *Veru*, or *spede* for the Englishe word inclineth closer to the Italian imitation : *Veruuersator*, Turnspet. He is called also VVaupe, of the naturall noise of his voyce *VVau*, which he maketh in barcking. But for the better and the redyer sounde, the vowell, u, is chaunged into the cōsonant, p, so y for waupe we say wappe. And yet I wot well that *Nonius* boroweth his *Baubari* of the natural voyce *Bau*, as the *Grœcians* doe their βωὐζειν of wau.

Now when you vnderstand this that *Saltare* in Latine signifieth *Dansare* in Englishe. And that our dogge therevpon is called a dannser and in the Latine *Saltator*, you are so farre taught as you were desirous to learne, and now suppose I, there remaineth nothing, but that your request is fully accomplished.

The winding vp of this worke, called the Supplement, &c.

THus (friend *Gesner*) you haue, not only the kindes of our countrey dogges, but their names also, as well in latine as in Englishe, their offices, scruices, diuersities, natures properties, that you can demaunde no more of me in this matter. And albeit I haue not satisfied your minde peraduēture (who suspecteth al speede in the performaunce of your requeste employed, to be meere delayes) because I stayde the setting fourth of that vmperfect pamphlet which, fiue yeares ago, I sent to you as a priuate friende for your own reeding, and not to be printed, and so made common, yet I hope (hauing like the beare lickt ouer my younge) I haue waded in this worke to your contentation, which delay hath made somewhat better and διντἰραι φρωντίδις, after witte more meete to be perused.

The ende of this treatise.

FINIS.

✿ *An Alphabeticall Index, declaring the*

D.

The Table.

The Table.

Y.

The ende of the Index.

¶ Faultes escaped
thus to b'amended.

In the last page of the Epistle Dedicatory, *Quæ* for *Qui.*

Page. 3. *Grecians* for *Græcians.*

Page. 28. *Canis Cultos* for *Canis Custos.*

Page. 38. *Britanica* for *Britannica.*

Other faultes we referre to the correction of
the Reader.

There bee also certaine *Accents* wanting in the Greeke words which,
because we had them not, are pretermitted ; so haue wee byn fayne to
let the Greeke words run their full length, for lacke of *Abbreuiations.*

Studio & industiæ,

Abrahami

Flemingi.

LONDON :

PRINTED BY A. BRADLEY, 170, STRAND, W C.

1880.

Catalogue

of

Practical Handbooks.

ANIMALS, BIRDS, &c.

BREAKING AND TRAINING DOGS:
Being Concise Directions for the proper Education, both for the Field and as Companions, of Retrievers, Pointers, Setters, Spaniels, Terriers, &c. By "PATHFINDER."
In cloth gilt, 5s., by post, 5s. 4d.

DISEASES OF DOGS:
Their Pathology, Diagnosis, and Treatment; to which is added a complete Dictionary of Canine Materia Medica; Modes of Administering Medicines; Treatment in cases of Poisoning, and the Value of Disinfectants. For the Use of Amateurs. By HUGH DALZIEL (Author of "British Dogs," &c.). NEW, REVISED, AND GREATLY ENLARGED EDITION.
In paper, price 1s., by post 1s. 1d.; in cloth gilt 2s., by post 2s. 2d.

BRITISH DOGS:
Their Varieties, History, Characteristics, Breeding, Management, and Exhibition. Illustrated with 52 Portraits of the Chief Dogs of the Day. By HUGH DALZIEL ("Corsincon," Author of "The Diseases of Dogs," "The Diseases of Horses," &c.), assisted by Eminent Fanciers. [May also be had in Divisions, as under]:
Bevelled boards, extra gilt, gilt edges, price 10s., by post, 10s. 6d.

DOGS USED IN FIELD SPORTS:
Their History, Varieties, Characteristics, &c. With nineteen full page Portraits of celebrated Dogs of the Day. (*Forming Division I. of "British Dogs.*")
In paper, price 3s., by post, 3s. 3d.

DOGS USEFUL TO MAN:
In other Work than Field Sports. Their History, Varieties, Characteristics, &c. With twenty-four full page Portraits of Leading Dogs of the Day. (*Forming Division II. of "British Dogs.*")
In paper, price 3s., by post, 3s. 3d.

HOUSE AND TOY DOGS:
Their History, Varieties, Characteristics, &c, Also the General Management of Dogs, and Breeding and Rearing. Illustrated with nine Portraits of Celebrated Dogs of the Day. (*Forming Division III. of "British Dogs.*")
In paper, price 2s., by post, 2s. 2d.

OF ENGLISHE DOGGES:
The Diversities, the names, the natures, and the properties. A Short Treatise written in latine by Iohannes Caius of late memorie, Doctor of Phisicke in the Universitie of Cambridge. And newly drawne into Englishe by ABRAHAM FLEMING, Student. *Natura etiam in brutis vim ostendit suam.* Seene and allowed. Imprinted at London by Rychard Iohnes, and are to be solde ouer against S. Sepulchres Church without Newgate. 1576. Reprinted verbatim. [Note.—This is the earliest book in the English language on the subject, and should be in the hands of all who take an interest in Dogs.]
In boards, price 2s. 6d., by post, 2s. 8d.

DISEASES OF HORSES:
Their Pathology, Diagnosis, and Treatment; to which is added a complete Dictionary of Equine Materia Medica. For the Use of Amateurs. By HUGH DALZIEL.
In paper, price 1s. 6d., by post, 1s. 8d.

PRACTICAL DAIRY FARMING:
A short Treatise on the Profitable Management of a Dairy Farm. Illustrated. By G. SEAWARD WITCOMBE.
In paper, price 1s. 6d., by post, 1s. 7d.

BOOK OF THE GOAT:
Containing Practical Directions for the Management of the Milch Goat in Health and Disease. Illustrated. By H. STEPHEN HOLMES PEGLER.
Cheap edition, in paper, price 1s., by post, 1s. 1d.

PIG KEEPING FOR AMATEURS:
A Practical Guide to the Profitable Management of Pigs. By G. GILBERT ("Gurth."
In paper, price 1s., by post, 1s. 1d.

STOCK KEEPING FOR AMATEURS:
A Manual on the Varieties, Breeding, and Management of Pigs, Sheep, Horses, Cows, Oxen, Asses, Mules, and Goats, and the Treatment of their Diseases. Designed for the use of Young Farmers and Amateurs. By W. H. ABLETT. Author of "Farming for Pleasure and Profit," "Arboriculture for Amateurs").
In cloth gilt, price 5s., by post, 5s. 4d.

RABBITS FOR PRIZES AND PROFIT:
Containing Full Directions for the proper Management of Fancy Rabbits in Health and Disease, for Pets or the Market; and Descriptions of every known Variety, with Instructions for Breeding good specimens. Illustrated. By the late CHARLES RAYSON. Edited by LEONARD U. GILL. [May also be had in two Parts, as under]:
In cloth gilt, price 2s. 6d., by post, 2s. 9d.

GENERAL MANAGEMENT OF RABBITS:
Including Hutches, Breeding, Feeding, Diseases and their Treatment, Rabbit Coverts, &c. Fully illustrated. (*Forming Part I. of "Rabbits for Prizes and Profit."*)
In paper, price 1s., by post, 1s. 1d.

EXHIBITION RABBITS:
Being Descriptions of all Varieties of Fancy Rabbits, their Points of Excellence, and how to obtain them. Illustrated. (*Forming Part II. of "Rabbits for Prizes and Profit."*)
In paper, price 1s., by post, 1s. 1d.

BOOK OF THE RABBIT:
A complete work on Breeding and Rearing all varieties of Fancy Rabbits, giving their History, Variations, Uses, Points, Selection, Mating, Managemen , and every other information. Illustrated with facsimiles of water-colour drawings specially prepared for this work, and numerous wood engravings. By Various Breeders and Exhibitors. Edited by LEONARD U. GILL, (Editor of "Rabbits for Prizes and Profit").
In extra cloth gilt, bevelled boards, gilt edges, price 12s. 6d., by post, 13s.

FERRETS AND FERRETING:
Containing Instructions for the Breeding, Management, and Working of Ferrets.
In paper, price 6d., by post, 7d.

FANCY MICE:
Their Varieties, Management, and Breeding. Illustrated.
In paper, price 6d., by post, 6½d.

FOREIGN CAGE BIRDS:
Containing Full Directions for Successfully Breeding, Rearing, and Managing the various Beautiful Cage Birds imported into this country. Beautifully Illustrated. By C. W. GEDNEY.
In cloth gilt, in two vols., price 8s. 6d., by post, 9s.; in extra cloth gilt, gilt edges, in one vol., price 9s. 6d., by post, 9s. 10d.

PARRAKEETS, PARROTS, COCKATOOS, LORIES, AND Macaws:
Their Varieties, Breeding and Management. (*Forming Vol. I. of "Foreign Cage Birds."*)
In cloth gilt, price 3s. 6d., by post, 3s. 9d.

WAXBILLS, FINCHES, WEAVERS, ORIOLES, AND Other Small Foreign Aviary Birds:
Their Varieties, Breeding, and Management. Beautifully illustrated. (*Forming Vol. II. of "Foreign Cage Birds."*)
In cloth gilt, price 5s., by post, 5s. 4d.

CANARY BOOK:
Containing Full Directions for the Breeding, Rearing, and Management of Canaries and Canary Mules; Formation of Canary Societies; Exhibition Canaries, their points and breeding; and all other matters connected with this fancy. Illustrated. By ROBERT L. WALLACE. [May also be had in two Parts, as follows]:
In cloth gilt, price 5s., by post 5s. 4d.; in extra cloth gilt, gilt edges, price 6s., by post, 6s. 4d.

GENERAL MANAGEMENT OF CANARIES:
Including Cages and Cage Making, Breeding, Managing, Mule Breeding, Diseases and their Treatment, Moulting, Rats and Mice, &c. Illustrated. (*Forming Part I. of the "Canary Book."*)
In paper, price 2s., by post, 2s. 2d.

EXHIBITION CANARIES:
Containing Full Particulars of all the different Varieties, their Points of Excellence, Preparing Birds for Exhibition, Formation and Management of Canary Societies and Exhibitions. Illustrated. (*Forming Part II. of the "Canary Book."*)
In paper, price 2s., by post, 2s. 2d.

FANCY PIGEONS:
Containing Full Directions for the Breeding and Management of Fancy Pigeons, and Descriptions of every known variety, together with all other information of interest or use to Pigeon Fanciers. Handsomely illustrated. By J. C. LYELL.
In extra cloth gilt, price 7s. 6d., by post, 8s.

POULTRY FOR PRIZES AND PROFIT:
Contains Breeding Poultry for Prizes, Exhibition Poultry, and Management of the Poultry Yard. Hand-omely Illustrated. By JAMES LONG.
In cloth gilt, price 2s. 6d., by post, 2s. 9d.

BREEDING POULTRY FOR PRIZES:
Containing full instructions for Mating Poultry to obtain the best results in each breed. Illustrated. (*Forming Part I. of "Poultry for Prizes and Profit."*)
In paper, price 6d., by post, 6½d.

EXHIBITION POULTRY:
Their Varieties, Characteristics, and Points of Excellence. Illustrated. (*Forming Part II. of "Poultry for Prizes and Profit."*)
In paper, price 1s., by post, 1s. 1d.

MANAGEMENT OF THE POULTRY YARD:
Including Hatching of Eggs, Rearing and Feeding, Houses and Runs, General Management, Diseases and their Treatment, Fattening, Poultry Farming, &c. Illustrated. (*Forming Part III. of "Poultry for Prizes and Profit."*)
In paper, price 1s., by post, 1s. 1d.

SUCCESSFUL CHICKEN REARING, A GUIDE TO.
Price, in paper, 6d., by post 6½d.

DUCKS AND GEESE:
Their Characteristics, Points, and Management. By VARIOUS BREEDERS. Splendidly illustrated.
In paper, price 1s. 6d., by post, 1s. 7d.

PRACTICAL BEE-KEEPING:
Being Plain Instructions to the Amateur for the Successful Management of the Honey Bee. Illustrated. Re-written and Enlarged. By FRANK CHESHIRE.
In cloth gilt, price 2s. 6d., by post, 2s. 9d.

BEE-KEEPING FOR AMATEURS:
Being a Short Treatise on Apiculture on Humane and Successful Principles. By THOMAS ADDEY (the Lincolnshire Apiarian).
In paper, price 6d., by post, 6½d.

PRACTICAL MECHANICS.

PATENTS, TRADE MARKS, AND DESIGNS:
A Practical Guide to Inventors and Manufacturers for Securing Protection under each of these heads. By ARCHIBALD CRAIG.
In cloth gilt, price 1s. 6d., by post, 1s. 8d.; in paper, price 1s., by post, 1s. 1d.

PRACTICAL ARCHITECTURE:
As applied to Farm Buildings of every description (Cow, Cattle and Calf Houses, Stables, Piggeries, Sheep Shelter Sheds, Root and other Stores, Poultry Houses), Dairies, and Country Houses and Cottages. Profusely Illustrated with Diagrams and Plans. By ROBERT SCOTT BURN.
In cloth gilt, price 5s., by post, 5s. 4d.

PRACTICAL BOAT BUILDING FOR AMATEURS:
Containing full Instructions for Designing and Building Punts, Skiffs, Canoes, Sailing Boats, &c. Fully illustrated with working diagrams. By ADRIAN NEISON, C.E. New Edition, revised and enlarged by DIXON KEMP (Author of "Yacht Designing," "A Manual of Yacht and Boat Sailing," &c.).
In cloth gilt, price 2s. 6d., by post, 2s. 8d.

ART OF PYROTECHNY:
Being Comprehensive and Practical Instructions for the Manufacture of Fireworks, specially designed for the use of Amateurs. Profusely Illustrated. By W. H. BROWNE, Ph.D, M.A., L.R.C.P. Second Edition.
In cloth gilt, price 2s. 6d., by post, 2s. 10d.

MINOR FIREWORKS:
Containing Instructions for the Manufacture of the Common and Simple Varieties of Fireworks. For the Use of Amateurs. Illustrated. By W. H. BROWNE, Ph.D., M.A., &c. (Author of "The Art of Pyrotechny").
In paper, price 1s., by post, 1s. 1d.

PRACTICAL FIREWORK MAKING FOR AMATEURS:
Being complete and explicit Directions in the Art of Pyrotechny, as applied to both the Major and Minor Fireworks, for the use of Amateurs and Beginners. By W. H. BROWNE, Ph.D., M.A., L.R.C.P., &c. Illustrated.
In cloth gilt, price 3s. 6d., by post 3s. 9d.

PRINTING FOR AMATEURS:
A Practical Guide to the Art of Printing; containing Descriptions of Presses and Materials, together with Details of the Processes employed, to which is added a Glossary of Technical Terms. Illustrated. By P. E. RAYNOR.
In paper, price 1s., by post 1s. 2d.

TURNING FOR AMATEURS:
Containing full Description of the Lathe, with all its working parts and attachments, and minute instructions for the effective use of them on wood, metal, and ivory. Illustrated with 130 first class wood engravings. Second Edition.
In cloth gilt, price 2s. 6d., by post, 2s. 9d.

CARPENTRY AND JOINERY FOR AMATEURS:
Contains full Descriptions of the various Tools required in the above Arts, together with Practical Instructions for their use. By the Author of "Turning for Amateurs," "Working in Sheet Metal," &c.
In cloth gilt, price 2s. 6d., by post, 2s. 9d.

WORKING IN SHEET METAL:
Being Practical Instructions for Making and Mending small Articles in Tin, Copper, Iron, Zinc, and Brass. Illustrated. Third Edition. By the Author of "Turning for Amateurs," &c.
In paper, price 6d., by post, 6½d.

WOOD CARVING FOR AMATEURS:
Containing Descriptions of all the requisite Tools, and full Instructions for their use in producing different varieties of Carvings. Illustrated.
In paper, price 1s., by post, 1s. 1d.

PRACTICAL MECHANICS FOR AMATEURS:
A Series of Treatises on Turning, Carpentry and Joinery, Working in Sheet Metal, Wood Carving, Firework Making, and Printing. Illustrated.
In Cloth gilt, price 10s. 6d., by post, 11s. 2d.

ORGANS AND ORGAN BUILDING:
Giving the History and Construction of the Modern Organ, and Descriptions of the most remarkable Instruments. With Important Specifications of celebrated Organs. Illustrated. By C. A. EDWARDS.
In cloth gilt, price 5s., by post, 5s. 4d.

TOYMAKING FOR AMATEURS:
Containing Instructions for the Home Construction of Simple Wooden Toys, and of others that are moved or driven by Weights, Clockwork, Steam, Electricity, &c. Illustrated. By JAMES LUKIN, B.A. (Author of "Turning for Amateurs.")
In cloth gilt, price 4s., by post, 4s. 4d.
Part I.—SIMPLE WOODEN TOYS, in paper, price 1s. 6d., by post 1s. 8d.
Part II.—CLOCKWORK, STEAM, and ELECTRICAL TOYS, in paper, price 2s.

MODEL YACHTS AND BOATS:
Their Designing, Making, and Sailing. Illustrated with 118 Designs and Working Diagrams. By J. DU V. GROSVENOR.   [In the Press.

POPULAR NATURAL HISTORY.

PRACTICAL TAXIDERMY:
A Manual of Instruction to the Amateur in Collecting, Preserving, and Setting-up Natural History Specimens of all kinds. Illustrated. By MONTAGU BROWNE.
In cloth gilt, price 3s. 6d., by post, 3s. 9d.

COLLECTING BUTTERFLIES AND MOTHS:
Being Directions for Capturing, Killing, and Preserving Lepidoptera and their Larvæ. Illustrated. Reprinted, with additions, from "Practical Taxidermy." By MONTAGU BROWNE (Author of "Practical Taxidermy").
In paper, price 1s., by post 1s. 1d.

POPULAR BRITISH FUNGI:
Containing Descriptions and Histories of the Principal Fungi, both Edible and Poisonous, of our Country. Illustrated. By JAMES BRITTEN, F.L.S., &c.
In cloth gilt, price 3s. 6d., by post, 3s. 9d.

BRITISH MARINE ALGÆ:
Being a Popular Account of the Seaweeds of Great Britain, their Collection and Preservation. Magnificently illustrated with 205 engravings. By W. H. GRATTAN.   In cloth gilt, price 5s. 6d., by post, 5s. 10d.

ZOOLOGICAL NOTES:
On the Structure, Affinities, Habits, and Faculties of Animals; with Adventures among and Anecdotes of them. By ARTHUR NICOLS, F.G.S., F.R.G.S. (author of "The Puzzle of Life, and How it Has Been Put Together," "Chapters from the Physical History of the Earth "). [In the press.

GUIDES TO GARDENING.

THE CHRYSANTHEMUM:
Its History, Varieties, Cultivation, and Diseases. By D. T. FISH.
In paper, price 6d., by post 7d.

GARDEN PESTS AND THEIR ERADICATION:
Containing Practical Instructions for the Amateur to Overcome the Enemies of the Garden. With numerous Illustrations of the perfect Insects and their Larvæ, which are particularly harmful to Garden Plants.
In paper, price 1s., by post, 1s. 1d.

THE HARDY FRUIT BOOK:
Consisting of a Series of Exhaustive Treatises on various Hardy Fruits grown in this country; giving the History, the most desirable Sorts, and the best Methods of Cultivation of each. Illustrated. By D. T. Fish. [May be had in Parts as follow]:

THE APPLE:
Its History, Varieties, Cultivation, Pruning, Training, Cropping, &c.
In paper, price 1s., by post, 1s. 1d.

THE PEAR:
Its History, Varieties, Cultivation, Pruning, Training, Cropping, &c.
In paper, price 1s. 6d., by post, 1s. 7d.

THE PEACH AND NECTARINE:
Their History, Varieties, Cultivation, Pruning, Training, Cropping, &c.
In paper, price 1s. 6d., by post, 1s. 7d.

THE APRICOT:
Its History, Varieties, Cultivation, Pruning, Training, Cropping, Diseases, &c.
In paper, price 1s., by post 1s. 1d.

THE PLUM:
Its History, Varieties, Cultivation, Pruning, Training, Cropping, &c.
In paper, price 1s., by post, 1s. 1d.

THE CHERRY AND MEDLAR:
Their History, Varieties, Cultivation, and Diseases.
In paper, price 1s., by post 1s. 1d.

THE FIG, MULBERRY, AND QUINCE:
Their History, Varieties, Cultivation, and Diseases.
In paper, price 1s., by post 1s. 1d.

THE WALNUT, CHESTNUT, AND FILBERT:
Their History, Varieties, and Cultivation.
In paper, price 1s., by post, 1s. 1d.

ORCHIDS FOR AMATEURS:
Containing Descriptions of Orchids suited to the requirements of the Amateur, with full Instructions for their successful Cultivation. With numerous beautiful Illustrations. By JAMES BRITTEN, F.L.S. (of the British Museum), and W. H. GOWER.
In cloth gilt, price 7s. 6d., by post, 7s. 10d.

ROSE GROWING FOR AMATEURS:
Being Practical Instructions for the successful Culture of Roses, with selections of the best varieties adapted to the requirements of the Amateur in Town or Country. By W. D. PRION.
In paper, price 1s. 6d., by post, 1s. 8d.

BULBS AND BULB CULTURE (Vols. I. and II.):
Being Descriptions, both historical and botanical, of the principal Bulbs and Bulbous Plants grown in this country, and their chief Varieties; with full and practical instructions for their successful Cultivation, both in and out of doors. Illustrated. By D. T. FISH. Vol. I. includes Parts I. and II., and Vol. II. Parts III. and IV., as named below.
In cloth gilt, price 2s. 6d., by post, 2s. 9d.

THE SNOWDROP, BULBOCODIUM, STERNBERGIA, Crocus, Colchicum, Tulip, and Hyacinth:
The best sorts, and their cultivation, indoors, under glass, and in the open border. Illustrated. (*Forming Part I. of "Bulbs and Bulb Culture."*)
In paper, price 1s., by post, 1s. 1d.

THE ANEMONE, THE NARCISSUS, THE LILY:
The best sorts, and their cultivation, indoors, under glass, and in the open border.
Illustrated. (*Forming Part II. of "Bulbs and Bulb Culture."*)
In paper, price 1s., by post, 1s. 2d.

THE GLADIOLUS, LACHENALIA, CYCLAMEN, RANUN-
culus, and Scilla or Squill (Star Hyacinth):
The best sorts, and their cultivation, indoors, under glass, and in the open border.
Illustrated. (*Forming Part III. of "Bulbs and Bulb Culture."*)
In paper, price 1s., by post, 1s. 1½d.

IXIAS, SPARAXIS, TRITONIAS, AND BABIANAS; IRIS,
Tiger Iris; Schizostylis Coccinea; and the Dahlia.
The best sorts, and their cultivation, indoors, under glass, and in the open
border. Illustrated. (*Forming Part IV. of "Bulb Culture."*)
In paper, price 1s., by post, 1s. 1d.

VINE CULTURE FOR AMATEURS:
Being Plain Directions for the successful growing of Grapes, with the means and
appliances usually at the command of amateurs. Illustrated. By W. J. MAY.
In paper, price 1s., by post, 1s. 1d.

PRUNING, GRAFTING, AND BUDDING FRUIT TREES:
Illustrated with ninety-three Diagrams. By D. T. FISH.
In paper, price 1s., by post, 1s. 1d.

VILLA GARDENING:
Being plain instructions for the Proper Laying-out, Planting, and Management
of Small Gardens; with lists of Trees, Shrubs, and Plants most suitable, and
thirteen Designs for small gardens. By W. J. MAY.
Cheap edition, in paper, price 1s., by post, 1s. 1d.

ROSE BUDDING:
Containing full Instructions for the successful performance of this interesting
operation. Illustrated. By D. T. FISH.
In paper, price 6d., by post, 7d.

GREENHOUSE MANAGEMENT FOR AMATEURS:
Descriptions of the best Greenhouses and Frames, with Instructions for Building
them; Particulars of the various Methods of Heating; lists of the most suitable
plants, with general and special cultural directions; and all necessary information
for the Guidance of the Amateur. Illustrated. By W. J. MAY (Author of "Vine
Culture for Amateurs," "Cucumber Culture for Amateurs," &c.).
In cloth gilt, price 3s. 6d., by post, 3s. 9d. In extra gilt, gilt edges, price 4s., by post, 4s. 3d.

ARBORICULTURE FOR AMATEURS:
Being Instructions for the Planting and Cultivation of Trees for Ornament
or Use, and selections and descriptions of those suited to special requirements as to
Soil, Situation, &c. By WILLIAM H. ABLETT (Author of "English Trees and
Tree Planting," &c.).
In cloth gilt, price 2s. 6d., by post, 2s. 8d.

CUCUMBER CULTURE FOR AMATEURS:
Including also Melons, Vegetable Marrows, and Gourds. Illustrated. By W. J. MAY.
In paper, price 1s., by post, 1s. 1d.

VEGETABLE CULTURE FOR AMATEURS:
Concise Directions for the Cultivation of Vegetables, so as to insure good crops, in
small Gardens, with lists of the best varieties of each sort. By W. J. MAY.
In paper, price 1s., by post 1s. 1d.

SPORTS AND PASTIMES.

COUNTRY POCKET BOOK AND DIARY, 1882:
For Reference and Registration. Full of facts and forms of the greatest value
and interest to Country Gentlemen and Sportsmen. Contents: Diaries and
Information on Shooting, Fishing, Hunting, Athletics, Football, Bicycling,
Coursing, Racing, Dogs, Poultry Exhibitions, Rowing, Swimming, Meteorology,
Cricket, Parliamentary Papers, &c., &c., with Pockets, Pencil, &c., complete.
Prices: In russia leather, 5s. 6d.; roan, 3s. 6d.; postage, 2d.

BICYCLES AND TRICYCLES OF THE YEAR:
Being a Chronicle of the New Inventions and Improvements for the present
Season, and forming a Permanent Record of the progress in the manufacture of
Bicycles and Tricycles. Designed also to assist intending purchasers in the choice
of a machine. Illustrated. By HARRY HEWITT GRIFFIN. (Published Annually.)
In paper, price 1s., by post, 1s. 1d.

THE BICYCLIST'S GUIDE TO MACHINES AND MAKERS:
Showing at a glance the construction and price of the principal machines in the market. By ROBERT EDWARD PHILLIPS, D.B.C., C.S.B.C., B.T.C.
In paper, price 6d., by post, 6½d.

PRACTICAL TRAPPING:
Being some Papers on Traps and Trapping for Vermin, with a chapter on general bird trapping and snaring. By W. CARNEGIE ("Moorman").
In paper, price 1s., by post, 1s. 1d.

PRACTICAL FISHERMAN:
Dealing with the Natural History, the Legendary Lore, the Capture of British Freshwater Fish, and Tackle and Tackle Making. Beautifully illustrated. By J. H. KEENE.
In cloth gilt, gilt edges, price 10s. 6d., by post, 11s.

NOTES ON GAME AND GAME SHOOTING:
Miscellaneous observations on Birds and Animals, and on the Sport they afford for the Gun in Great Britain, including Grouse, Partridges, Pheasants, Hares, Rabbits, Quails, Woodcocks, Snipe, and Rooks. By J. J. MANLEY, M.A. (Author of "Notes on Fish and Fishing"). Illustrated with Sporting Sketches by J. TEMPLE.
In cloth gilt, 400 pp., price 7s. 6d., by post 7s. 10d.

PRACTICAL BOAT BUILDING AND SAILING:
Containing Full Instructions for Designing and Building Punts, Skiffs, Canoes, Sailing Boats, &c. Particulars of the most suitable Sailing Boats and Yachts for Amateurs, and Instructions for their proper handling. Fully Illustrated with Designs and Working Diagrams. By ADRIAN NEISON, C.E., DIXON KEMP, A.I.N.A., and G. CHRISTOPHER DAVIES.
In One Volume, cloth gilt., price 7s.; by post, 7s. 6d.

BOAT SAILING FOR AMATEURS:
Containing Particulars of the most Suitable Sailing Boats and Yachts for Amateurs, and Instructions for their Proper Handling, &c. Illustrated with numerous Diagrams. By G. CHRISTOPHER DAVIES (Author of "The Swan and her Crew," &c.).
In cloth gilt, price 5s., by post 5s. 3d.

PRACTICAL PHOTOGRAPHY:
Being the Science and Art of Photography, both Wet Collodion and the various Dry Plate Processes, Developed for Amateurs and Beginners. Illustrated. By O. E. WHEELER. [May also be had in parts as under]:
In cloth gilt, price 4s., by post, 4s. 4d.

WET COLLODION PROCESS:
The Art of Photography by this process, developed for Amateurs and Beginners.
(*Being Part I. of "Practical Photography."*)
In paper, price 1s., by post, 1s. 2d.

DRY PLATE PHOTOGRAPHY:
The Art of Photography by this Process developed for Amateurs and Beginners.
(*Being Part II. of "Practical Photography."*)
In paper, price 1s., by post, 1s. 2d.

PHOTOGRAPHIC MISCELLANEA:
(*Being Part III. of "Practical Photography."*)
In paper, price 1s., by post 1s. 2d.

THE PHOTOGRAPHER'S POCKET BOOK:
Containing Register for nearly 1000 Negatives. Compiled by O. E WHEELER (Author of "Practical Photography").
Prices: In cloth, 3s.; in leather 3s. 6d.; by post, 2d. extra.

ARTISTIC AMUSEMENTS:
Being Instructions for a variety of Art Work for Home Employment, and Suggestions for a number of Novel and Saleable Articles for Fancy Bazaars. Illustrated. Contents are given in Series I. and II. following.
In cloth gilt, price 2s. 6d., by post, 2s. 8d.

SERIES I. OF "ARTISTIC AMUSEMENTS."
Colouring Photographs, Imitation Stained Glass, Decalcomanie, Queen Shell Work, Painting on China, Japanese Lacquer Work, Stencilling.
In paper, price 1s., by post, 1s. 1d.

SERIES II. OF "ARTISTIC AMUSEMENTS."
Painting Magic Lantern Slides, Menu and Guest Cards, Spatter Work, Picture and Scrap Screens, Frosted Silver Work, Picture Cleaning and Restoring, Illuminating and Symbolical Colouring.
In paper, price 1s., by post, 1s. 1d.

CHINA PAINTING:
Its Principles and Practice. By WALTER HARVEY. Illustrated.
In paper, price 1s., by post, 1s. 1d.

LEATHER WORK BOOK:
Containing Full Instructions for Making and Ornamenting articles so as to successfully imitate Carved Oak; specially written for the use of Amateurs. By ROSA BAUGHAN. Illustrated.
In cloth gilt, price 2s. 6d., by post, 2s. 9d.

CARDS AND CARD TRICKS:
Containing a brief History of Playing Cards: Full Instructions, with Illustrated Hands, for playing nearly all known games of chance or skill, from Whist to Napoleon and Patience, and directions for performing a number of amusing Tricks. Illustrated. By H. E. HEATHER.
In cloth gilt, price 5s., by post, 5s. 4d.

SLEIGHT OF HAND:
Being Minute Instructions by the Aid of which, with proper practice, the Neatest and most Intricate Tricks of Legerdemain can be successfully performed. Illustrated. By EDWIN SACHS. [May also be had in two parts as follow]:
In cloth gilt, price 5s., by post, 5s. 4d.

DRAWING ROOM MAGIC:
Being Conjuring Tricks suited to Beginners, and for display in drawing rooms. Illustrated. (*Forming Part I. of "Sleight of Hand."*)
In paper, price 2s., by post, 2s. 2d.

GRAND OR STAGE MAGIC:
Being Instructions for the Performance of more intricate and showy conjuring tricks, and suited to public display. Illustrated. (*Forming Part II. of "Sleight of Hand."*) In paper, price 2s., by post, 2s. 2d.

GUIDES TO PLACES.

THE UPPER THAMES:
From Richmond to Oxford: A Guide for Boating Men, Anglers, Pic-nic Parties, and all Pleasure Seekers on the River. Arranged on an entirely new plan. Illustrated with Specially Prepared Engravings of some of the most Beautiful Scenery and Striking Objects met with on the Thames.
In paper, price 1s., in cloth, with elastic band and pocket, 2s., postage 2d.

WINTER HAVENS IN THE SUNNY SOUTH:
A complete Handbook to the Riviera, with a notice of the new station, Alassio. Splendidly Illustrated. By ROSA BAUGHAN (Author of "Indications of Character in Handwriting," "The Northern Watering Places of France").
In cloth gilt, price 2s. 6d., by post, 2s. 8d.

THE DICTIONARY OF WATERING PLACES, Seaside and Inland, at Home and Abroad:
Contains Routes, Climate, and Season, Waters, Recommended for, Scenery, Objects of Interest, Amusements, Churches, Doctors, Hydropathic Establishments, Hotels, House Agents, Newspapers, &c., with MAP OF BRITISH WATERING PLACES, Seaside and Inland, and the Routes thereto. In cloth, price 4s., by post, 4s. 3d.

May also be had in Parts, as follows, price 2s. each,

Part I., BRITISH WATERING PLACES, both Inland and Seaside, in England, Ireland, Scotland, Wales, and the Islands.
Part II., FOREIGN WATERING PLACES, Seaside and Inland, including the Spas, the Swiss Lakes, and the Continental Centres.

SEASIDE WATERING PLACES:
Being a Guide to Persons in Search of a Suitable Place in which to Spend their Holidays, on the English and Welsh Coasts. New and Revised Edition, with Descriptions of over 140 Places.
In paper, price 2s., by post, 2s. 3d.

MAP OF THE SEASIDE AND INLAND WATERING Places of the British Isles:
Showing the railway and steamboat communications, the central points, and various places of interest to tourists, in addition to all the Watering Places mentioned in the British Section of the "Dictionary of Watering Places" and in "Seaside Watering Places." Size of plate 15in. by 14½in. Coloured, price 6d., by post 7d.; plain, price 3d., by post 4d.

NORTHERN WATERING PLACES OF FRANCE:
A Guide for English People to the Holiday Resorts on the Coasts of the French Netherlands, Picardy, Normandy, and Brittany. By ROSA BAUGHAN (Author of "Winter Havens in the Sunny South," &c.).
In paper, price 2s., by post 2s. 2d.

MISCELLANEOUS.

ENGLISH POTTERY AND PORCELAIN:
A Manual for Collectors. Being a Concise Account of the Development of the Potter's Art in England. Profusely Illustrated with Marks, Monograms, and Engravings of characteristic Specimens. New Edition. [May also be had in Parts as under]: In cloth gilt, price 3s. 6d., by post. 3s. 8d.

ENGLISH POTTERY:
Giving the History of the most famous and valued descriptions of English Pottery, with illustrations of specimens, marks, and monograms, &c. (*Forming Part I. of "English Pottery and Porcelain."*)
In paper, price 1s. 6d., by post, 1s. 7d.

ENGLISH PORCELAIN:
Giving the History of the most famous and valued descriptions of English Porcelain, with illustrations of specimens, marks, and monograms, &c. (*Forming Part II. of "English Pottery and Porcelain."*)
In paper, price 1s. 6d., by post, 1s. 7d.

ENGLISH, SCOTCH, AND IRISH COINS:
A Manual for Collectors; being a History and Description of the Coinage of Great Britain, from the Earliest Ages to the Present Time, with Tables of Approximate Values of Good Specimens. Profusely Illustrated.
In cloth gilt, price 5s., by post, 5s. 4d.

CHARACTER INDICATED BY HANDWRITING:
With Illustrations in support of the Theories advanced, taken from Autograph Letters of Statesmen, Lawyers, Soldiers, Ecclesiastics, Authors, Poets, Musicians, Actors, and other persons. By R. BAUGHAN.
In cloth gilt, price 2s. 6d., by post 2s. 9d.

CHURCH FESTIVAL DECORATIONS:
Comprising Directions and Designs for the Suitable Decoration of Churches for Christmas, Easter, Whitsuntide, and Harvest. Illustrated.
In paper, price 1s., by post 1s. 1d.

ARTISTIC FLOWER DECORATIONS:
For Ball Rooms, Halls, Passages, Dinner and Supper Tables; with Directions for making Bouquets, Buttonholes, Hair Sprays, &c. Illustrated. By B. C. SAWARD.
In paper, price 2s., by post, 2s. 2d.

TUNING AND REPAIRING PIANOFORTES:
The Amateur's Guide to the Practical Management of a Piano without the intervention of a Professional. By CHARLES BABBINGTON.
In paper, price 6d., by post 6½d.

DICTIONARY OF NEEDLEWORK:
An Encyclopædia of Plain and Fancy Needlework; the History of the various Work; details of the Stitches employed; the method of working the materials used; the meaning of Technical Terms; and other information bearing on the subject. Plain, practical, complete, and magnificently Illustrated. By S. F. A. CAULFEILD and B. C. SAWARD, assisted by various ladies.
In monthly parts, price 1s., by post, 1s. 1½d.

HONITON LACE BOOK:
Containing Full and Practical Instructions for Making Honiton Lace. With numerous illustrations.
In cloth gilt, price 3s. 6d., by post, 3s. 9d.

PRACTICAL DRESSMAKING:
Being Plain Directions for Taking Patterns, Fitting on, Cutting out, Making up, and Trimming Ladies' and Children's Dresses. By R. MUNROE.
In paper, price 1s., by post, 1s. 1d.

TOILET MEDICINES:
A Scientific Manual on the Correction of Bodily Defects, and the Improvement and Preservation of Personal Appearance; together with Formulæ for all the Special Preparations Recommended. By EDWIN WOOTON, B.Sc. (Paris).
In cloth gilt, price 2s. 6d., by post, 2s. 9d.

SICK NURSING AT HOME:
Being Plain Directions and Hints for the Proper Nursing of Sick Persons, and the Home Treatment of Diseases and Accidents in case of sudden emergencies. By S. F. A. CAULFEILD.
In paper, price 1s., by post, 1s. 1d. In cloth, price 1s. 6d., by post 1s. 8d.

HINTS TO UNTRAINED TEACHERS:
Being Directions and Suggestions for the Assistance of Parents and others engaged
in Home Education. By JANE ASCHAM.
In paper, price 6d., by post 7d.

STOCK AND SHARE INVESTMENTS:
Being Explanations for the General Reader of the Nature and Quality of the
different Classes of Securities dealt in on the Stock Exchange. By ALBERT
SHARWOOD.   In paper, price 1s., by post, 1s. 1d.

CATALOGUE OF LADIES' AND CHILDREN'S DRESS
Patterns (Illustrated):
Comprising Ladies' Dresses, Mantles, Underlinen, Girls' and Boys' Costumes,
Children's Underlinen, Ladies' Caps, Dressing Jackets, &c. This list is added to
week by week, and at present contains nearly four hundred of the newest and
most seasonable designs. Post free on application.

PIANOFORTES, £19 10s.
AMERICAN ORGANS, £9 5s.
HARMONIUMS, £5 15s.

Perfect in Tone and Touch. Elegant Walnut Cases. Every instrument warranted to
stand any extreme climate. Shippers and Dealers supplied.
Before deciding on purchasing, write for a descriptive Price List and Testimonials to
G. LINSTEAD, Manager,

COBDEN PIANOFORTE COMPANY,
18, EVERSHOLT STREET, CAMDEN TOWN, LONDON.

Read the following Testimonials, selected from many hundreds:—
Darley Ripley, Leeds, 25 Jan., 1878.—DEAR SIR,—The American Organ is to hand, and
is a really good instrument. The tone is all that can be desired, and the appearance is
far beyond my expectation. I am a teacher of music, and will recommend them.—Yours
truly,   J. C. BRADBURY.
British and Foreign Bible and Book and Tract Depot, 25, Church-street, Sheffield,
26 Oct., 1877.—DEAR SIR,—The Piano came safely. I am very much pleased with it as a
sweet and brilliant-toned instrument, and beautifully polished. My friends who have
tried it like it very much. It is also handsome in appearance. I shall recommend you
wherever I can.—I am, yours, &c.   E. RHODES.
Shields Daily News Office, 11, Howard-street, North Shields, 7 March, 1878.—DEAR SIR.
—The Harmonium has arrived, and gives great satisfaction. Your guarantee as regards
quality is quite fulfilled. We are glad that we can speak so favourably respecting it, and
it speaks very well in your favour when being used.—Yours respectfully,
                                                    WHITECROSS and YORKE.
64, Union-street, Maidstone, 27 Oct., 1879.—DEAR SIR,—About a year since I purchased
one of your American Organs. My family and friends are delighted with its superior
finish and brilliant tone: in a word, it is a "GEM." I could bear similar testimony of
your Pianofortes, and temperance friends requiring an instrument for the family circle
will do well to give your establishment a trial.—Most respectfully yours,
                                                    G. H. GRAHAM.

THE UNIVERSAL HOUSEHOLD REMEDIES!!!

HOLLOWAY'S PILLS & OINTMENT

These excellent **FAMILY MEDICINES** are invaluable in the
treatment of all ailments incidental to every **HOUSEHOLD.**
The **PILLS PURIFY, REGULATE** and **STRENGTHEN** the
whole system, while the **OINTMENT** is unequalled for the cure
of Bad Legs, Bad Breasts, Old Wounds, Sores, and Ulcers. Pos-
sessed of these **REMEDIES**, every Mother has at once the means
of curing most complaints to which herself or Family is liable.

*N.B.—Advice Gratis at 533, Oxford Street, London, daily between the hours
of Eleven and Four, or by letter.*

ROWLAND'S TOILET ARTICLES,

20, HATTON GARDEN, LONDON.

ROWLAND'S ODONTO

Or PEARL DENTIFRICE is of inestimable value in preserving and beautifying the teeth, strengthening the gums, and giving a pleasant fragrance to the breath ; it eradicates tartar from the teeth, prevents and arrests decay, and polishes and preserves the enamel, to which it imparts a pearl-like whiteness. Its unprecedented success for more than half a century shows the universal favour in which it is held, while the fact of its being entirely free from any acid or mineral ingredients constitutes it the safest and purest tooth powder ever used. To prevent fraud the genuine Odonto has a 3d. Government stamp on the box. Ask for Rowland's Odonto.

ROWLAND'S MACASSAR OIL

Is universally in high repute for its unprecedented success during the last 80 years in promoting the growth, restoring, improving, and beautifying the human hair. It prevents hair from falling off or turning grey, strengthens weak hair, cleanses it from scurf and dandriff, and makes it beautifully soft, pliable, and glossy. For children it is especially recommended, as forming the basis of a beautiful head of hair, while its introduction into the nursery of Royalty is a sufficient proof of its merits. Sold in usual four sizes.

ROWLAND'S KALYDOR,

An Eastern botanical preparation, perfectly free from all mineral or metallic admixture. It is distinguished for its extremely bland, purifying, and soothing effects on the skin ; while by its action on the pores and minute secretory vessels, it promotes a healthy tone, allays every tendency to inflammation, and thus effectually dissipates all redness, tan, pimples, spots, freckles, discolourations, and other cutaneous visitations. The radiant bloom it imparts to the cheek, the softness and delicacy which it induces of the hands and arms, its capability of soothing irritation, and removing cutaneous defects, render it indispensable to every toilet. Gentlemen after shaving will find it renders the skin soft, smooth, and pleasant. Of all Chemists, at 4s. 6d. Avoid cheap spurious imitations. Sold by all dealers in perfumery.

The Theatrical and Music Hall Profession,

Amateur Theatricals, Fancy Dress Balls. &c.

Moustaches, 6d. and 1s.; whiskers and moustache, 1s., imperials, 6d.; full beards and moustaches, 1s. 6d., 2s., and 2s. 6d.; niggers' wigs, 2s., 3s. 6d., with spring to fly up, 4s. 6d.; niggers' black, 1s.; clowns' wigs, 8s.; pantaloons', with beard, complete, 14s.; scratch wigs, all colours, 7s. 6d.; dress wigs, all colours, 12s. 6d.; spirit gum, 6d. and 1s.; grease paints, 7d. per stick, all sent post free.

The largest stock of Wigs and Makes-up in the world.

HUNDREDS OF SECONDHAND WIGS FOR SALE.

Amateur Theatricals attended with Wigs, Makes-up, and a competent man, terms, 10s. 6d. to 21s., according to the pieces played and the distance from London.

WIGS LENT ON HIRE.

C. H. FOX,

18, RUSSELL STREET, COVENT GARDEN, London,

And 60, SAUCHIEHALL STREET, GLASGOW.

GOLDEN FLUID,

THE VERY BEST MADE.

Patronised by all the principal *artistes* and ladies of fashion, will impart the most beautiful golden tint to the hair in a few applications. Quite harmless.

Expressly prepared for and sold by

C. H. FOX, 19, Russell Street, Covent Garden, London,

And 60, SAUCHIEHALL STREET, GLASGOW,

In bottles: Pints, 12s.; half pints, 6s.; gills, 3s. Imperial measure.

LUXURIANT AND BEAUTIFUL HAIR.

"Look on this picture."   **"And on this."**

LATREILLE'S EXCELSIOR LOTION.

Celebrated among all classes of society all over the world as the only real producer

WHISKERS AND MOUSTACHIOS,

AND CURER OF BALDNESS.

Price 2s. 6d. per bottle. Can be had of any chemist, through Barclay, Sanger, Newbery, Edwards, Sutton, Thompson, Hovenden, Maw and Co., or any other Wholesale Chemist, or direct from the proprietors, LATREILLE and Co., Walworth, London, on remitting Post-office Order or Stamps.

CAUTION.—Be careful to ask for Latreille's Excelsior Lotion, and refuse anything else that may be offered, as the enormous success, extending over twenty years, has led to many useless imitations, which can only disappoint. The title "EXCELSIOR LOTION" is a registered Trade Mark, to copy which will incur criminal prosecution.

www.ingramcontent.com/pod-product-compliance
Lightning Source LLC
Chambersburg PA
CBHW021427090426
42742CB00009B/1297